D1571035

LYCIAN TURKEY

AN ARCHAEOLOGICAL GUIDE

LYCIAN TURKEY

AN ARCHAEOLOGICAL GUIDE

GEORGE E. BEAN

LONDON/ERNEST BENN LIMITED
NEW YORK/W. W. NORTON AND COMPANY INC.

First published 1978 by Ernest Benn Limited
25 New Street Square, Fleet Street, London EC4A 3JA
& Sovereign Way, Tonbridge, Kent TN9 1RW
and W. W. Norton and Company Inc.
500 Fifth Avenue, New York, N.Y. 10036

Distributed in Canada by
The General Publishing Company Limited, Toronto

Printed in Great Britain

British Library Cataloguing in Publication Data

Bean, George Ewart
 Lycian Turkey.
 1. Lycia—Antiquities
 I. Title
 915.64   DS156.L8

ISBN 0–510–03205–2
ISBN 0–393–05708–9 (U.S.A.)

Foreword

THE PRESENT VOLUME fills the gap left by my three previous books, *Aegean Turkey, Turkey's Southern Shore*, and *Turkey beyond the Maeander*; the four together now cover the whole of the south-west corner of Turkey from Pergamum to Alânya.

Lycia is still the least accessible and least visited part of this region, even though there has been a great change in recent years. When I first visited the Xanthus valley in 1946, the country was really remote. Tractors were unknown, and every man simply grew on his own patch of land enough to feed his family through the year; no one bothered to market his produce in Fethiye; the two-days trek each way with a donkey was not worthwhile. When I asked, 'What do you do in the winter?', the answer was, 'We sit'. It is not so now; bus and lorry transport and modern agricultural machinery have produced a transformation. Commerce was previously confined to timber and the oranges of Finike; now there is a flourishing market in tomatoes on the plain of Demre. Roads and hotels are sometimes backward; there is good accommodation in Fethiye, considerably less good in Finike, Kaş, and Elmalı. The dirt roads vary greatly in quality, but at least it is possible to travel by car all the way from Fethiye to the east coast, and a jeep brings many more places within reach.

Looking back over twenty-five years of exploration in Anatolia, I remember with most pleasure my journeys in Lycia. They were certainly strenuous, even to the point of exhaustion often enough, but the country has, at least for me, a fascination not equalled elsewhere. The scenery is impressive, often spectacular, and seen by moonlight is out of this world; and the ancient monuments, especially of course the tombs, have a quality of their own.

Since Sir Charles Fellows removed the Xanthian marbles to the British Museum no excavation was done in Lycia for a century and a quarter, and most of the sites are still untouched save for illicit digging by the villagers. In 1962 the French began a thoroughgoing excavation of Xanthus and the Letoum which is still in progress, and of late work has also been done at Myra, Limyra, and Arycanda. So, although it is now seven years since I left Turkey, not much change is likely to have occurred in the meantime. The descriptions of the sites in this book are all at first hand, with the exception of Arneae, which I have never been able to visit.

It may be well to draw travellers' attention to the new and severe law in Turkey concerning antiquities. Since 1973 all finds must be delivered by the owner of the property to the appropriate museum, and may not be bought, sold, or exported. Any foreigner found in possession of any antiquity, whether bought or found, is at once suspected of intending to take it out of the country, and if brought to the notice of the police, is liable to arrest and imprisonment. Souvenir-hunting is accordingly illegal and strongly to be discouraged.

Here again I have written primarily for the traveller, presupposing an interest in antiquities rather than any special knowledge, and have not hitherto included references for the individual statements. It has, however, been represented to me that scholars who may on occasion find the books useful would welcome such references, and I have this time included a list of passages from the ancient authorities. For modern discussions the Bibliography must suffice.

As before, the photographs were taken by me, and the text figures are by my wife. In dealing with Aperlae I have been greatly assisted by Mr Robert S. Carter of Melina, Washington, United States, who has courteously allowed me to make use of his investigations on the site. I have also to acknowledge with gratitude the advice of Professor Oliver Gurney and Professor Martin Harrison.

It is perhaps worthwhile to repeat again the rules for pronunciation of Turkish names. Vowels are pronounced as in German, consonants as in English, with these exceptions: c = English j, ç = English (t)ch; ş = English sh; ğ after soft vowels = English y, after hard vowels it merely lengthens them. The dotless ı is peculiar to Turkish, but most nearly resembles the indeterminate vowel-sound in the English bor*ough* or *a*way. y is always a consonant, and h is always pronounced.

Contents

CONTENTS   9

List of Plates

[*In one section between pages 156 and 157*]

List of Illustrations in Text

Publishers' Note

Professor Bean died before production of this his last work began. The Publishers wish to thank Mrs Jane Bean, Professor Martin Harrison, and Mr Alan Hall for their kind help in seeing the book through the press.

Professor Harrison also translated Wolfgang W. Wurster's article on Tlos, Apollonia, and Candyba, 'Antike Siedlungen in Lykien', which has been of great help in bringing the accounts of these three sites up to date. Mr Hall advised on the latest excavations at Oenoanda. The index was prepared by Mr Douglas Gardner.

Glossary

Acroterium. An ornament placed at one of the angles of a pediment.

Agora. The market-place.

Analemma. The end wall of the cavea of a theatre.

Ashlar. Masonry of squared blocks laid in horizontal courses.

Cavea. The auditorium of a theatre.

Coffer. An ornamental panel recessed in a vault or ceiling.

Cuneus. One of the wedge-shaped blocks of seats in a theatre.

Deme. A subdivision of a city's territory; a village.

Dentil Frieze. A frieze consisting of a row of alternate square projections and square spaces.

Diazoma. A horizontal passage across the cavea of a theatre.

Ethnic. An adjective formed from a place-name, usually denoting a citizen of that place.

Exedra. A semicircular recess or alcove furnished with a bench.

Fascia. One of three (or sometimes two) horizontal stepped bands on an architrave or other architectural member.

Hellenistic Period. The period from the time of Alexander to that of Augustus (approximately the last three centuries B.C.).

Hyposorium. Basement chamber of a tomb, commonly intended for relatives or dependants.

Orthostates. Blocks set upright, generally to form the lowest course of a wall.

Parodoi. Side entrances to a theatre, between the cavea and the stage-building.

Pediment. A triangular space like a gable, set over a colonnade or other architectural feature.

Proscenium. The front wall of a stage.

Stele. A narrow slab of stone set upright and generally bearing writing or decoration or both.

B

Stoa. A covered portico or gallery, for protection against sun and rain.

Stylobate. The stone pavement on which a row of columns stands.

Triglyph Frieze. A frieze consisting of groups of three upright bars separated by plain blocks called metopes.

CHAPTER ONE

Historical

LYCIA MAY BE ROUGHLY DEFINED as the country lying
south of a line drawn from Köyceğiz to Antalya. In its main
natural features it is remarkably symmetrical; first and
foremost, the two mighty masses of Akdağ, the ancient
Massicytus, on the west, and Bey Dağı, the ancient Solyma, on
the east; both are over 10,000 feet high. To the west of Akdağ
is the valley of the Xanthus, with beyond it the minor range of
Cragus and Anticragus; to the east of Bey Dağı is the valley of
the Alakır (ancient name uncertain), with beyond it the minor
range of Tahtalı Dağı. These rivers are the largest in the
country; the even longer Dalaman Çayı to the north-west is not
genuinely in Lycia. The northern part of the country consists
of a comparatively level plateau consistently over 3,000 feet
above the sea.

So mountainous a land was bound to be thinly and unevenly
inhabited; the total population in antiquity has been estimated
at a mere 200,000. All the chief cities are on the coast or in the
Xanthus valley; this latter was the true heart of Lycia. In
summer the day temperature is regularly over 90°F; the modern
inhabitants, unless they have business to detain them, leave
their villages when the crops are in in June and make their way
to the high ground to the north, and there is reason to believe
that the ancients did the same (see below, p. 50). Between May
and mid-September rainfall is scanty; in the central region
there is no running water and the people are dependent on
wells; it is not uncommon for these to dry up before the time
comes for the summer migration. Altogether a hard land, and
it had a hardy folk.

Among the various races of Anatolia the Lycians always held
a distinctive place. Locked away in their mountainous country,

they had a fierce love of freedom and independence, and resisted strongly all attempts at outside domination; they were the last in Asia Minor to be incorporated as a province in the Roman Empire. They had a language of their own which is still imperfectly understood, written in characters many of which are peculiar to it. They had an instinct for union and federation, and formed a Lycian nation when elsewhere the Greek world was made up of individual city-states perpetually at enmity with one another. They had customs of their own and a style of funerary architecture which is quite unique.

Where did they come from, and when? The Greek tradition is recorded by Herodotus, who says they came originally from Crete; when Minos and his brother Sarpedon quarrelled for the power, Minos was victorious and Sarpedon with his followers crossed to Asia and settled in Lycia, which was then called Milyas, driving out the Solymi who were in occupation. For a time they kept their name of Termilae (which is still used by their neighbours), but when Lycus, son of Pandion king of Athens, expelled by his brother Aegeus, came to join Sarpedon, they took from him their name of Lycians. The traditional date for Pandion as recorded by the Parian Marble[1] is the early thirteenth century, whereas Minos and Sarpedon are placed in the latter half of the fifteenth century. These dates are of course quite unreliable, and the chronology is further confused by a later Minos in the time of Lycus and Aegeus and a later Sarpedon in the time of the Trojan War (late thirteenth century).

Chronologically much surer ground is afforded by the Hittite records, which refer a number of times to a nation of the Lukka, who can be no other than the Lycians. We learn that the Lukka lands were conquered by the Hittites in the reign of Suppiluliumas in the mid-fourteenth century, though they were not securely held but were often in rebellion. Further evidence comes from the tablets found at Tel-el-Amarna in Egypt, where certain Lukki are mentioned among a group of sea-raiders about the same time. For the location of the Lukka lands the indications are mostly vague; they seem to have been close neighbours

[1] An inscription set up on the island of Paros consisting of a table of dates from the earliest mythological times until 264 B.C.

of the Arzawa somewhere to the west or south-west of the
Hittite capital Hattusas. This, combined with the description of
them as sea-raiders, would naturally place them in Caria and/or
Lycia. There is, however, one more precise piece of evidence.
The records mention a city of Dalawa in the Lukka lands; if,
as seems virtually certain, this is the same as the Lycian Tlawa,
that is Tlos, in the Xanthus valley, the location of the Lukka
in Lycia in the fourteenth century is established. Furthermore,
Dalawa is associated in the records with the city of Hinduwa,
which is likely to be identical with the classical Candyba.

There seems accordingly nothing to prevent us from accepting
the settlement of Lycia, perhaps towards 1400 B.C., by Cretans
under Sarpedon. According to the historian Ephorus they came
first to Caria, where they founded the city of Miletus, calling it
after the Cretan city of the same name. Another tradition
asserted that the Carian city of Idrias, later Stratoniceia, was
the first city founded by the Lycians; if this has any historical
basis, it will mark the passage of the Lycians southward from
Miletus to their eventual home. Herodotus' story of the name
Lycian being taken from the Athenian Lycus, improbable in
itself, is obviously to be rejected.

FIG. 1 Districts of Asia Minor

Not so his assertion that the Lycians were originally called Termilae. Not only is this repeated by other ancient writers, but it is strikingly confirmed by the inscriptions in the native language, which refer to them always as TRM̃MILI, never as Lycians. The Greek inscriptions, on the contrary, never use the name Termilae; even the Xanthian Obelisk (see below, pp. 57–8), about 400 B.C., in its Greek portion speaks of Lycians. The Lycian inscriptions date to the late fifth and fourth centuries, or barely later than Herodotus' time. Not merely the neighbours, therefore, but the Lycians themselves continued to use the name Termilae. It is not, of course, rare for a people to call themselves by a name different from that used by others; the modern Greeks and Germans are obvious examples; nevertheless, it is possible that the Termilae are to be distinguished, as later incomers, from the Lukka or Lycians. If so, the language of the inscriptions should more properly be called Termilic.

This language (which for present purposes may be called Lycian) is known only from the inscriptions and the coin-legends; the latter, however, offer merely a series of names of dynasts. The inscriptions comprise 153 texts previously known and a number of new ones from the excavations at the Letoum not yet published. They are written in an alphabet of twenty-nine letters, of which nineteen are Greek (in a few cases with a different pronunciation), the others mostly peculiar to Lycian. These last appear to have been invented by the Lycians to represent sounds used in Lycian but not in Greek. Exactly what these sounds were has not been determined with certainty, but it is generally agreed that they include two nasal vowels, ã and ẽ, as well as two sonants m̃ and ñ. The words are usually, though not consistently, divided by a double point (:). On the stones the letters were commonly coloured, often alternately red and blue, though the colours have now in most cases disappeared.

The great majority of the texts consists of epitaphs; the principal exceptions are the Xanthian Obelisk, which contains a good deal of historical and other matter, and a new trilingual text from the Letoum referring to the institution of a religious cult. The epitaphs are comparatively simple, with constantly recurring formulae: so-and-so built this tomb for his wife and

sons and/or others; if anyone violates it, he shall pay a stated
penalty. These are fairly easy to understand; the longer texts,
on the other hand, remained until recently for the most part
unintelligible. The language has many Indo-Germanic features.
The nouns and verbs are inflected (declined and conjugated),
though the inflexions are confined to the endings, the stem
remaining unchanged; there are no irregular verbs. The
vocabulary seems to have its closest affinity with Etruscan, a
language which came originally from western Asia Minor.

FIG. 2 Lycian Epitaph
ebẽññẽ prñnawu mẽn. e prñnawatẽ hanadaza
hrppi ladi ehbi setideime
'Hanadaza built this building for his wife and
    sons'

For the understanding of the language a number of bilingual
inscriptions have given help, and the new trilingual from the
Letoum will surely afford more. Meanwhile scholars, in particular Professor Hans Stoltenberg, have offered interpretations,
certain or conjectural, of most of the individual words, and it
may be said that the general sense of the Lycian inscriptions is
now in large part understood.

Herodotus observes that the Lycian customs are partly
Cretan, partly Carian; they have, however, he says, one custom
which is peculiar to them and unique among mankind: they
reckon their lineage not by the father's but by the mother's
side. Ask a Lycian who he is and he will name his mother and
his mother's mothers. Moreover, the children of a female
citizen, even from a slave, are reckoned legitimate, whereas
those of a male citizen from a foreigner or a concubine are
illegitimate. Lycians, like Greeks, had only one name, and it was
the practice all over the Greek world to use the father's name
as a surname, like the English Johnson or Richardson. We
should naturally therefore expect to find the Lycian matriarchal

system reflected in the inscriptions. In fact it is simply not so. Both in the Lycian and in the Greek inscriptions a man calls himself son of his father in the usual way. It is true that there are cases, at least in the later periods, where the mother's name is used; but there is no reason to suppose that these are other than cases of unknown paternity, a phenomenon by no means confined to Lycia. It is also true that it is not always possible to be sure of the gender of a Lycian name; but in every case where the parent's sex is certain, it is male. How are we to explain this contradiction? There must surely be some historical grounds for Herodotus' statement. He wrote towards the end of the fifth century, which is just about the date of the earliest Lycian inscriptions. Was he describing a custom which formerly prevailed in Lycia, wrongly supposing that it still survived? Was he attributing to the Lycians the custom of some other nation? Or are we to imagine that the Lycians in their private lives used the matriarchal system, but on their public monuments followed the practice universal elsewhere? The mystery has never been solved.

The earliest appearance of the Lycians in Greek literature is in Homer's *Iliad*, where they fight as allies of the Trojans, coming 'from distant Lycia and the eddying Xanthus'; their commanders Sarpedon and Glaucus play a not undistinguished part among the minor heroes. Homer is now generally agreed to have composed towards 700 B.C.; by the sixth century the Lydian kings had conquered the whole of Asia Minor west of the river Halys with the exception of the Lycians and the Cilicians. The last king of Lydia, Croesus, fell to the Persians in 546 B.C., and his kingdom passed to them. The Persians were not willing to leave the Lycians in freedom, and sent an army under their general Harpagus to subdue them; after a desperate resistance the Lycians submitted to superior force (see below, p. 50). Persian rule was mild, requiring little more than the payment of tribute, and the country was left to be governed by its own dynasts; by the end of the century these were striking silver coins in their own names.

In 480 B.C., when Xerxes assembled his huge force for the conquest of Greece, the Lycians contributed fifty ships to his fleet; the men, says Herodotus, wore breastplates and greaves, with bows of cornel wood, unwinged arrows of reed, javelins, goat-skins over their shoulders, and feathered hats on their heads, also daggers and scimitars. Of their exploits in the war we hear nothing.

Following the Persian defeats at Salamis and Plataea the Athenians established their maritime league, known as the Delian Confederacy, to include the cities of the western shores of Asia Minor. Payment of tribute was required from each city, and the records of these payments, beginning in 454 B.C., are largely preserved. Lycia is scantily represented; Phaselis pays regularly, but was not properly a Lycian city at that time; Telmessus pays once, in 446, and in the same year appears an entry 'Lycians and fellow-contributors', with a tribute of ten talents. Who these fellow-contributors may have been is not clear; perhaps 'Lycians' means in effect 'Xanthians',[2] and the associates are the other Lycian cities. In any case, Lycian participation in the Delian Confederacy can only have been short-lived. Such as it was, it seems to have been due to the expedition of the Athenian general Cimon in 469, in which he is said to have cleared the coast of the Persian garrisons which were still in occupation at that date.[3]

When the Peloponnesian War ended in 404 with the complete defeat of Athens by Sparta, the Delian Confederacy ceased to exist. Sparta took over, but had not the qualities for managing an overseas empire, and Lycia fell back under Persian domination. During all this time the Lycian dynasts continued to issue their silver coinage. In the early fourth century the Persian satrap of Caria was Mausolus, an energetic and ambitious man who took advantage of the slack Persian rule to make himself in effect an independent despot; in addition to the whole of Caria he extended his claims to Lycia also. The Lycians resisted under their dynast Pericles; only Phaselis, still not a true Lycian city, accepted Mausolus, and even concluded a treaty with him. Pericles, treating Phaselis as an enemy, submitted her to a blockade.[4]

Any pretensions of Mausolus' successors to control of Lycia

[2] As in Herodotus; see below, p. 49.
[3] See *Turkey's Southern Shore*, Appendix I.
[4] See *Turkey's Southern Shore*, p. 153.

ended with the arrival of Alexander in 333. After the reduction of Halicarnassus, Alexander proceeded to Lycia, where he made a treaty with Telmessus, then, crossing the Xanthus, received the surrender of Pinara, Xanthus, and some thirty minor cities. Phaselis showed herself especially friendly; she offered him her submission together with a golden crown, and Alexander stayed some time in the city, incidentally lending her his troops to subdue some troublesome neighbours. He then moved on into Pamphylia.

After Alexander's death Lycia came into the power of his general Ptolemy, who had established himself as king of Egypt. Ptolemaic control continued for about a hundred years, and it was during this period that the Lycian language died out and was replaced by Greek; the rule of the dynasts had come to an end with Pericles and the cities adopted Greek constitutions. In 197 B.C. the country was taken from the Ptolemies by Antiochus III, king of Syria; Phaselis, Limyra, Andriace, Patara, and Xanthus are specially mentioned as having been captured by him.[5] He was shortly afterwards defeated by the Romans at the battle of Magnesia; in the settlement which followed in 189 Lycia, with the exception of Telmessus, was given to the Rhodians, who had supported Rome. The Lycians, intolerant as ever of foreign domination, resisted bitterly, claiming that they had been given to Rhodes not as subjects but as allies; the Rhodians claimed complete suzerainty, and for ten years there was fierce fighting. In 177 the Lycians, no longer able to hold out, sent an embassy to Rome to complain of the harshness of Rhodian rule. Roman relations with Rhodes had by this time cooled, and the Senate gave the Lycians a favourable reply, to the effect that they were supposed to be merely friends and allies of the Rhodians. Encouraged by this, the Lycians took up arms again, and hostilities continued for another six years, but by 171 the Lycians were again exhausted. In 167, however, the Senate decided to put an end to Rhodian control of Caria and Lycia and declared these countries free. Only one result of the Rhodian rule in Lycia was of any permanence: Phaselis, a Rhodian colony by origin, was at last included in Lycia with her western neighbours.

[5] For the case of Xanthus see below, p. 51.

Some time in the second century, perhaps near the beginning, two men, Lysanias and Eudemus, seized control of the city of Xanthus, carried out executions, and attempted to set up a tyranny. A campaign of the League forces was needed to suppress them and restore the situation. Shortly afterwards Eudemus made a second attempt at Tlos, and again the League forces had to be called in. It is evident that at the time of these events the Lycian League was in full vigour and ready to act in the defence of liberty.

In the long period of freedom after 167 B.C. the Lycian League came into prominence. It was not a new phenomenon; the Lycians had always an instinct for union and collaboration, and even under the dynasts of the fourth century the Lycian inscriptions refer repeatedly to the payment of fines to the 'Federal Treasurer of the Termilae'. Concerning this early federation we have no precise information. Of the later League, on the other hand, we have a detailed account by Strabo, supplemented by what we learn from the inscriptions. Strabo says there are twenty-three cities possessing the vote; they 'come together from each city' to a federal congress at a city chosen for the occasion; the most important cities have three votes each, the less important two, and the others one. Taxes and other public burdens are allocated in these proportions to the various cities. At the congress a Lyciarch is chosen, then the other League officials and panels of judges; minor magistrates and jurors in the federal courts are elected from each city in numbers proportional to its voting power. Formerly the congress decided questions of war, peace, and alliance, but now these decisions, save in special cases, naturally rest rather with the Romans. This account is in general well substantiated by our other information; it is, however, unsatisfactory in one respect, the nature of the 'congress'. The inscriptions, which are of course unassailable evidence, make no mention of a 'congress', but rather of two bodies, a Council and an Assembly, the latter generally styled electoral. From his account of its functions it seems Strabo's 'congress' must be the Assembly, and that he errs in omitting the Council. For the composition of the congress his words 'they come together from the cities' are certainly vague, and here again the inscriptions help to fill in the picture.

They make it clear that the Assembly was not, as it normally was in a Greek city, a primary assembly of the whole body of the citizens, but consisted of a limited number of delegates from the individual cities, determined in each case by the city's voting power. This system of representative government, with privileges and obligations in direct ratio to the city's classification, is the outstanding feature of the Lycian League.

Strabo's figure of twenty-three voting cities is astonishingly low. He had his information from Artemidorus, who wrote about 100 B.C., and it presumably refers to the situation at that time. Pliny, in the first century A.D., says there were formerly seventy cities in Lycia, but only thirty-six in his time. About forty whose names and sites are beyond doubt are discussed in the present volume, and many other small places are known which were probably or certainly not cities. Strabo's figure may be brought nearer to Pliny's if we suppose that his twenty-three refers not to individual cities but rather to voting units in the 'congress'; in a number of cases several of the smaller cities were united in a 'sympolity' and presumably shared a single vote. Such unions, headed by Aperlae, Acalissus, and Arneae, will be mentioned below. According to the same Artemidorus there were six cities possessing the maximum of three votes; four of these, Xanthus, Patara, Pinara, and Tlos, are in the Xanthus valley; central Lycia is represented by Myra and eastern Lycia by Olympus. No examples of two-vote cities are quoted, and none were known until the recent discovery of an inscription at Bubon recording the promotion of that city, in the second century A.D., from the two-vote class to the three-vote (see below, p. 164).

After the grant of freedom in 167 B.C. we hear little of Lycian affairs until the first Mithridatic War; the formation of the Roman province of Asia in 129 left Lycia untouched. In 88 the Pontic king Mithridates VI attacked and overran western Asia Minor; Roman administration had been so unsatisfactory that most places welcomed him as a liberator, but Lycia was among the few that resisted. Mithridates sent his officers to subdue it, and the Lycians had much to endure; the king himself made only one brief appearance at Patara (see below, p. 84), and Lycia was not effectively occupied. The war ended in 84 with the king's defeat by Sulla, and in the subsequent settlement the Romans showed their appreciation of the Lycians' loyalty by confirming their freedom and enlarging their territory by the addition of the three northern cities of Bubon, Balbura, and Oenoanda (see below, p. 162).

During the Roman civil wars of the first century B.C. the Lycians had again to suffer from the depredations of Brutus and Cassius, the 'tyrannicides' responsible for the murder of Julius Caesar in 44. The Lycian reluctance to contribute to Brutus' resources resulted in the capture and destruction of Xanthus (see below, pp. 51–3). Upon their defeat at Philippi in 42 by Antony and Octavian, Antony received the East as his share of the Roman world, and he too confirmed the freedom of Lycia, which thus remained as the only part of Asia Minor not incorporated in the Roman sphere of power. This state of affairs came at last to an end in A.D. 43, when Claudius joined Lycia with Pamphylia as a Roman province. This was not, however, quite the last of Lycian freedom, which was given back for a short while by Nero (A.D. 54–68), until Vespasian (A.D. 69–79) finally restored the composite province on a lasting basis.

Even under the Empire the Lycian League continued to function. Questions of war and peace, as Strabo observes, were naturally left to the Romans, but internal affairs, justice, and security, were still controlled by the League officials, who continued to be regularly appointed. The country was prosperous, money was plentiful, and huge fortunes could be amassed by private citizens; some of these, like Jason of Cyaneae and Opramoas of Rhodiapolis, made lavish gifts of money not only to their own cities, but also to many others in Lycia. At the same time most of the cities remained small; a total population of 200,000 gives an average of only some 5,000 for each city.

Although joined in a single province, Lycia and Pamphylia were an ill-assorted pair; the nature of the two countries and the character of the inhabitants were quite unlike. They naturally shared a Roman governor, but in practice each functioned separately. Each had its own magistrates headed by a Lyciarch or Pamphyliarch and managed its affairs with little or no regard for the other. Not that this mattered; the composite province

continued quite happily until it was finally split up by
Diocletian in the early fourth century. At this time too the
boundary of Lycia was extended to the north-west to include
the Carian city of Caunus; Calynda had been added to the
province at the time of its formation.

Nowhere in Anatolia is there a better opportunity to appre-
ciate the native culture than in Lycia. Here as elsewhere the
early buildings have been overlaid by those of the Hellenistic
and especially the Roman periods; but the Lycian tombs, for
which the country is famous, are in many cases earlier than the
time of Alexander, and are moreover frequently adorned with
sculptures. Many are still in excellent preservation.

These early tombs fall into four distinct classes, generally
called pillar-tombs, temple-tombs, house-tombs, and sarcophagi. The pillar-tombs (Pll. 10, 18, 35) are usually reckoned to
be the earliest and are peculiar to Lycia. They consist of a
rectangular pillar set on a base, with a grave-chamber at the top
surmounted by a wide cap-stone. This is the least common type
and seems to be confined to the western part of the country. The
temple-tombs (Pll. 2, 59) are not specifically Lycian, and differ
little from those of Caunus and other parts of Anatolia. They
have simply the façade of a temple, with two columns in antis,
usually in the Ionic order, an epistyle, and a pediment. A porch
leads through by a door to the grave-chamber, a plain room
with stone benches on which the dead were laid. The house-
tombs are in imitation of wooden houses, in one, two, or
occasionally three storeys; the square beam-ends are left
projecting. There is normally a row of round or square beam-
ends above the door; later these develop into a dentil frieze.
There is sometimes, but not always, a pediment above, and in
a few cases (Pl. 34) this has the shape of a pointed ('Gothic')
arch. The interior is similar to that of the temple-tombs.
Sarcophagi are of course one of the commonest forms of tomb
all over the world, but the early Lycian type is distinctive. It
is generally remarkable for its height, and is in three parts, a
base, a grave-chamber, and a crested 'Gothic' lid. The base is
commonly used as a second grave-chamber (hyposorion),
destined for the owner's slaves or dependants. On pillar-tombs
sculpture is confined, when it occurs at all, to the sides of the

grave-chamber at the top; the well-known example is the 'Harpy Tomb' at Xanthus (Pl. 14). House-tombs are often decorated with reliefs on the walls, in the pediment, and sometimes on the adjoining rocks; the most famous case is the 'Painted Tomb' at Myra (Pll. 72–6). Sarcophagi too are very frequently ornamented with reliefs, mostly on the sides and crest of the lid, but also in some cases on the grave-chamber itself (Pl. 55). In the Roman period the sarcophagi become much smaller and simpler, and the lid is rounded, though still with a crest. In addition to these four characteristic types there are in Lycia many other forms of tomb, some very striking; examples will be found in the following pages.

Splendid tombs, both rock-cut and of masonry, are found in most parts of Asia Minor, though nowhere in such abundance as in Lycia. Veneration for ancestors, amounting even to ancestor-worship, was almost universal in the ancient world. At Olympus in eastern Lycia two tombs carry letter-oracles where the response is conceived as given by the ancestor;[6] and in general much care was taken for the preservation of the tomb from damage or misuse. Epitaphs commonly end with the imprecation of a curse and/or a pecuniary fine for violation, and in Lycia we sometimes find the tomb under the care of a body called the *mindis* (MIÑTI in Lycian), apparently a committee of relatives charged with its protection. Fines for violation were in general payable to the city treasury, or in Roman times to the Imperial chest, the amount being fixed by the owner; he would pay a certain percentage of the chosen sum to the city officials, who would be responsible for convicting the offender and collecting the fine. In the Lycian inscriptions of the fourth century, however, we find a different system in use. The owner makes over the tomb to the *mindis*, who assume responsibility for its care; for this privilege he pays a modest fee, normally three staters.[7] Later, in the Greek inscriptions, much less is heard of the *mindis*; the city takes over, and by Roman times the system familiar elsewhere was in normal operation in Lycia also.

[6] See *Turkey's Southern Shore*, pp. 172–3.
[7] For an example of the *mindis* in action see below, p. 111.

CHAPTER TWO

The West Coast

THE ROAD FROM MUĞLA to Fethiye is scenically among the most beautiful in Turkey, owing chiefly to the splendid Carian pine-forests. It is also quite comfortably passable for a private car. A night-stop at Köyceğiz is not unattractive, if only for the lovely view over the lake. South of Köyceğiz the road crosses low and mainly level country as far as Dalaman, then turns sharply eastward and climbs high into the mountains, with fascinating glimpses of the sea by Göcek far below. This is the border country between Caria and Lycia. There is then a winding descent to the plain of Fethiye.

After passing the turning to Caunus the road, in about 6 miles, crosses by a modern bridge over the wide stony bed of the Dalaman Çayı. This is the ancient Indus, a very considerable river. Pliny says that it rises in the hills above Cibyra and receives as tributaries sixty perennial rivers and more than a hundred torrents. The first statement is correct; it does in fact rise south of Cibyra and flows for a good hundred miles to the sea, bearing today at least five different names in its various parts. The sixty perennial affluents, however, are certainly an exaggeration, though the map suggests that the hundred torrents may not be far from the mark.

Some 6 miles beyond the bridge is the village, formerly a *nahiye*, of Dalaman, notable only for a large State Farm. The village is now officially Karaçalı, but the familiar name is Dalaman. From here a pleasant excursion can be made to the large medieval site on the coast at Baba Dağ to the south-west. The road is dead flat across the plain, but there are two rivers to be crossed, and the traveller should know in advance how he proposes to manage. The Dalaman Çayı is usually fordable on horseback in summer, though not always without difficulty. The other stream, the Sarısu, is much less considerable; there is an *iskele* at its mouth where a boat is normally available.

The site itself is remarkably extensive and utterly deserted among the woods. The very numerous buildings, many of them in good preservation, are of inferior masonry and clearly of medieval date. Among them are a Christian church with apse and aisles, a high fortification wall, and a reservoir. Near the centre of the site is a large pond holding water even through the summer. It is probable that these ruins represent the medieval town of Prepia mentioned in the Italian portolans. At the same time there is evidence that an ancient town previously stood on the site. At its northern end is a rectangular fortress of square blocks which appears Hellenistic, and near the centre, especially between the pond and the reservoir, are a number of column-drums and other ancient stones, one bearing an inscription in honour of the emperor Julian. The name of this earlier town remains uncertain; the most probable suggestion is perhaps Pisilis, which Strabo seems to place between Calynda and Caunus.

Near the Sarısu landing-stage, a short distance offshore, is the small island of Baba Adası. This is crowned by a remarkable pyramidal structure, of which about half is preserved, built entirely of brick. It is in two storeys, the upper consisting of a circular room divided into four compartments by cross-walls; at the point where these cross is a round brick pillar three feet in diameter. The building has been variously understood as a mausoleum or a lighthouse; in view of the divided upper storey the latter suggestion appears more probable.

Just 4 kilometres, about $2\frac{1}{2}$ miles, beyond Dalaman an abundant spring issues on the right of the road beside a disused coffee-house. On a hill directly above this are the ruins of an ancient city which general opinion, including the present writer's, accepts as Calynda, though it is not actually identified by coins or inscriptions. The place is now called Kozpınar. Calynda was a city that lived its good days early. In 480 B.C. it supplied a single ship to Xerxes' fleet at Salamis, but this had the misfortune to be rammed and sunk by a ship of its own side commanded by the Carian queen Artemisia.[1] In the Delian

[1] For this curious incident see *Turkey beyond the Maeander*, p. 103.

C

Confederacy Calynda (in the form Claÿnda) paid a tribute twice
as large as that of Caunus. But as Caunus increased in importance Calynda correspondingly declined. Until 200 B.C. it was
still an independent city, but before 164 must have fallen under
Caunian control, since in that year it is said to have revolted
from Caunus and to have been given by the Roman Senate to
Rhodes. By the first century A.D. it was probably incorporated
in Caunus, but when the province of Lycia-Pamphylia was
finally established by Vespasian, Calynda, unlike Caunus, was
included in the Lycian League. Until then it had been reckoned
as Carian. As a member of the League the city was eligible for
a donation of 9,000 denarii from the millionaire Opramoas of
Rhodiapolis.

The hill at Kozpınar is of no great height; it is ascended by
a gentle slope on the west, the other sides being much steeper
or even precipitous. The upper part is encircled by a fortification
wall of polygonal masonry from 7 to 9 feet thick; the style
varies, but in part is of the 'coursed polygonal' variety which
dates to the early Hellenistic period. It stands in places up to
3 or 4 metres in height, but this is partly due to a late addition
in roughly squared blocks with cement. At the north corner is
a tower or small fort of good regular Hellenistic masonry,
divided into two chambers; it has a small door with a 'corbelled'
arch, formed by cutting the top course of the jambs obliquely
and closing the gap with a cap-stone. In the interior the whole
site is strewn with vast masses of building-stones, cut or uncut;
foundations of houses are discernible, but nothing is standing.
Great tales are told by the locals of the treasures of gold and
silver found on the site, and a good deal of illicit digging has
been done, but as usual none of the treasures are forthcoming.

The ancient evidence for placing Calynda on the map
consists of two passages, from Strabo and from Pliny. Strabo
says it is sixty stades, about $6\frac{1}{2}$ miles, from the sea; from
Kozpınar to the coast is 6 miles. Pliny records in order from
south to north: Crya, the river Axon, the town of Calynda, the
river Indus. On the map the first river after Crya is the Kargın
Çayı, a modest stream which passes close under the Kozpınar
site; between this and the Dalaman Çayı (Indus) there is no
ancient site. It seems almost inevitable, therefore, that the Axon

is the Kargın Çayı and that Calynda stood on it; in this case
Strabo's figure leads exactly to Kozpınar.

From Kozpınar the road continues eastward. Near the village
of Inlice, at a point just beyond the sign marking 'Fethiye
29 km.', close beside the road on the left, is an interesting tomb
cut in a rocky knoll. It is in the east face of the rock, and the
traveller going towards Fethiye must look back in order to see
it; from the other direction it is in full view. Rather unusually,
the tomb is in the Doric order. Three steps lead up to the porch,
which has two columns between pilasters; the columns are of
one piece with the tomb, cut from the rock. That on the right
is reduced to a foot or two at the top. Much of the Doric
ornamentation survives on the right—a triglyph frieze with a
dentil frieze above and mutules below. The pediment carried
three acroteria, of which that on the right is lost. There is no
inscription. The entrance to the main chamber is broken wide
open; the interior is a single room with stone benches round all
three sides on which the corpses were laid, and a flat, rather
rough roof. As a whole the tomb does not appear to be very
highly finished.

A little further on the attentive traveller may just discern,
high up in the hills to the left, a group of pigeon-hole tombs cut
in the hillside; they appear as tiny black squares. These mark
the site of the city of Daedala. Here again the identity is not
proved by inscriptions or coins, but the position agrees with the
ancient notices and is generally accepted. The site requires a
considerable effort to reach, and has in fact very rarely been
visited. It is known as Inlice Asarı. The steep acropolis hill is
surrounded on three sides by a wall of respectable ashlar
masonry; the west side is too precipitous to need a wall. On the
summit is a small fort. Also on the acropolis are rock-cut steps,
foundations of houses, and a circular stucco-coated cistern 5 feet
in diameter. A lower summit to the east was also included in the
city. But the principal remains are tombs. Three of these are
typical Lycian rock-tombs, and there are a few sarcophagi, but
most are of simple pigeon-hole type, cut in the rock-face and in
many cases quite inaccessible. These are especially numerous to
the west of the acropolis.

Strabo gives Daedala as marking the boundary between Caria and Lycia, and both he and Livy describe it as belonging to the Rhodian Peraea.[2] This is confirmed by an inscription found on the island of Tersane in the gulf of Fethiye, but stated to have come from a tomb at Daedala. It is a dedication by a Rhodian governor of the second century B.C., and the form of the wording shows that he was functioning on territory actually incorporated in the Rhodian state, not merely subject to Rhodes. No other such territory is known between here and the bay of Marmaris. There is some uncertainty whether the stone came from the Doric tomb by the roadside described above or from one of the Lycian tombs in the city itself; but in any case it appears that there was around Daedala an isolated enclave of the incorporated Rhodian Peraea.[3]

From Göcek an excursion may be made to the islands of the gulf of Fethiye (ancient Glaucus Sinus), of which Tersane is the largest. Here there was formerly a prosperous Greek village, but it is now deserted following the exchange of populations after the First World War. Ancient remains include a ruined watch-tower and a handsome built tomb partially preserved. It is possible, though quite unproved, that the ancient name of Tersane was Telandria, an island on which, according to Pliny, there was a town which had already perished in his day. On most of the other islands, or islets, there are various remains of the Byzantine age, but they are not of much account.

More interesting is the site on the west coast of the gulf at a spot called Taşyaka (formerly Charopia) to the north-west of Tersane. Near the shore is a group of temple-tombs a good deal damaged but remarkable because one of them carries an inscription not in Lycian but in Carian. As this language is not yet understood, it remains unknown what Carian dignitary was buried here. There are also some pigeon-hole tombs in the cliff-face. From the shore a rock-cut stairway led up the steep hill

[2] That is, Rhodian territory on the mainland.

[3] The matter of the inscription is not free from uncertainty. The statement that the stone came from a tomb on the mainland may not be reliable; it is a dedication to Good Fortune and Aphrodite, which a governor would hardly set up in a tomb. It must have come originally from some other place altogether.

to a tiny acropolis on the summit, barely 40 yards long and half as wide. It is enclosed by an early wall of mixed ashlar and polygonal masonry. In the interior are the foundations of a tower or small fort some 30 by 20 feet, and a large cistern. These scanty remains almost certainly represent the city of Crya. Yet again no inscriptions or coins have proved the identity, but the position agrees exactly with the notice in the *Stadiasmus*[4] which places it a little over 5 miles north of Lydae. Very little is in fact heard about Crya in the ancient writers. Pliny calls her 'Crya of the fugitives', but the reason for this curious title is not known. She is said to have possessed islands in the gulf, two of which are named as Carysis and Alina, but it is quite impossible to identify these. Crya was never more than a very modest city, and her citizens are very rarely met with in the inscriptions, so that a small site like that at Taşyaka seems perfectly suitable.

In the hill country to the north and east of Göcek are a great number of small ancient sites, but they are hard to reach, mostly unidentifiable, and unrewarding when reached.

[4] A kind of ancient portolan, listing the places along the shores of the Mediterranean, with a note of the distances between them. It was composed probably in the first century B.C.

CHAPTER THREE

Telmessus

THE SITE OF TELMESSUS at Fethiye has always been known. Tucked away in the south corner of the gulf, facing north, the town is hot in summer, though seldom unbearably so. In the summer of 1957 it suffered very severely from the earthquake that affected much of south-western Turkey. Apart from the buildings which were founded on the rocky slopes, virtually everything was laid flat; the débris of the town was swept up and thrown into the sea to form a new quay and esplanade. Among the general devastation the only thing that remained standing was the well-known Lycian sarcophagus beside the present municipal building; its lid had shifted a few inches. That there was no loss of life on this occasion was due to the prescience of the Kaymakam of Fethiye. The first shock was mild, but knowing that a more severe one was likely to follow, he sent round criers warning the people to leave their homes.

Nothing is known of the origin of Telmessus; although five inscriptions in the Lycian language have been found there, when the city first appears in history, she was not reckoned a part of Lycia. So in the fifth century in the tribute-lists of the Delian Confederacy Telmessus and the Lycians are listed separately; and in the fourth century we find the Lycians under their dynast Pericles fighting against the Telmessians, besieging them and reducing them to terms. The result of this may have been that Telmessus was then brought into Lycia, since the geographer who passes under the name of Scylax, writing in the same century, reckons the city as Lycian.

When Alexander arrived in the winter of 334–333 B.C., he made a peaceable agreement with the Telmessians, who joined him readily. Not long afterwards, however, Nearchus the Cretan, one of his trusted 'Companions' whom he had appointed satrap of the region, was obliged to recapture the city from a certain Antipatrides who had gained control of it. The two men were old friends, and Nearchus asked permission to leave in the city a number of captive women singers and boys that he had with him. When this was granted, he gave the women's musical instruments to the boys to carry, with daggers concealed in the flute-cases; when the party was inside the citadel, the prisoners' escort took out the weapons and so seized the acropolis. This is described by the historian as a stratagem; others might call it sharp practice.

In 240 B.C. Telmessus was presented by Ptolemy III to another Ptolemy, son of Lysimachus; and at the settlement in 189 B.C. after the battle of Magnesia (see above, p. 26) it was given by the Romans to Eumenes of Pergamum, but 'the lands which had belonged to Ptolemy' were allowed to remain in his hands. So far as we know, Telmessus continued in the Pergamene kingdom until that came to an end in 133 B.C.; it would then naturally be included in the Roman province of Asia. In 88 B.C. we hear that the Rhodians received help 'from the Telmessians and from the Lycians', implying that the city was not then included in Lycia. Later, certainly under the Empire and perhaps earlier, Telmessus was a normal member of the Lycian League. In the eighth century the city's name was changed to Anastasiupolis in honour of the Byzantine emperor Anastasius II; by the following century this too gave way to the name Makri, which in its turn was supplanted in the present century by Fethiye.

There is some evidence that divination was practised at Telmessus, and many tales are told of the Telmessian seers. There was, however, a second city of the same name in Caria where lived a famous priestly family of soothsayers,[1] and most of the reported cases are to be referred to them. It was said, for example, that while Alexander was besieging Halicarnassus, he took a midday siesta, and that a swallow came and fluttered round and round his bed, uttering abnormally loud cries and persisting until he awoke. Alexander thereupon consulted the seer Aristandrus of Telmessus, who declared that the portent foretold a plot against the king by one of his friends, which,

---

[1] See *Turkey beyond the Maeander*, p. 122.

however, would be brought to light. He explained that the swallow is a tame bird, friendly to man, and more garrulous than any other. Since the Carian Telmessus was only 7 miles from Halicarnassus, it is likely that Aristandrus lived there rather than at Fethiye.

Hardly anything now remains of the ancient city apart from the tombs; these, however, include some of the finest specimens of their kind. The principal group is just outside the town on the east, cut in the hillside facing north and west; they are reached by a stepped path recently constructed. The path leads directly to the most splendid and best known of all the tombs, the Tomb of Amyntas (Pl. 2). This is conspicuous from the plain below and from close to gives a great impression of size. It is of the temple-type, in the Ionic order. Four steps lead up to the porch with two columns between pilasters; half-way up the left-hand pilaster is inscribed, in letters of the fourth century B.C., the name of Amyntas son of Hermapias. The man in question is quite unknown. At the top of each pilaster is a row of three rosettes. Above is the pediment, with three acroteria, two of which are damaged; below is a dentil frieze. The door to the main chamber has four panels with imitation iron studs; the bottom right panel, originally closed with a sliding stone slab, has been broken open by robbers. The interior is a single chamber with a flat, rather rough roof and three separate benches along the sides. In the cliff-face further to the left are numerous other tombs; two of these are temple-tombs similar to that of Amyntas, and little less impressive. That on the left may be reached by an active man, but the other is more or less inaccessible. The lowest tombs are smaller, of house type in two or three storeys, and the rest mere pigeon-holes, unreachable without apparatus.

In and around the town are many more tombs, some rock-cut, others of sarcophagus type. A particularly fine specimen of the latter kind, perhaps the finest in all Lycia, now stands beside the municipal building (Pl. 4). A hundred years ago it was standing in the sea; the water-level, after rising since antiquity, has evidently fallen in recent times. It gives an impressive sense of solidity. It has a double front in two storeys, with square imitation wooden house-beams, and a lid of 'Gothic'-arch shape.

Both sides of the lid and of the surmounting crest carry reliefs showing rows of warriors. The ends of the lid are divided into four panels.

The acropolis hill of Telmessus rises at the back of the town; it is occupied chiefly by a medieval castle attributed to the Knights of St John. Beyond a few inscriptions built into the walls, and some undatable cisterns, the interior contains nothing ancient. In the east face of the hill is a pair of rock-tombs similar in type to that of Amyntas, but much smaller and simpler. On the west side facing north is a hollow which seems to have been the site of one of the two theatres which Telmessus possessed, but it is now very much cut up and contains nothing that particularly belongs to a theatre. At the top of the hollow is a small rock-tomb of house-type. The larger theatre stood close to the shore on the west side of the town; Fellows in 1838 described it as 'in tolerable preservation', and Spratt a few years later called it 'very perfect', but no vestige of it now remains.

CHAPTER FOUR

Excursions from Fethiye

CADYANDA

Twelve miles north-east of Fethiye, at Üzümlü, is the site of Cadyanda. The road is quite good apart from one or two rough patches, but is, or was in 1972, wrongly signposted where it branches off the main road. From Üzümlü there is a long and steep climb to the city, from one and a half to three hours according to age and activity. A guide may be had at Üzümlü.

Cadyanda, Kadawañti in Lycian, was never other than an obscure city. It is mentioned only once in the ancient writers, and that in a garbled passage where it has only recently been recognized. Pliny's manuscripts, listing the cities of Lycia, have *Ascandiadalis*, *Amelas*, two places quite unknown elsewhere. In this corruption Kalinka was the first to recognize *Cadyanda, Lissa*. From its termination -anda the name is evidently of high antiquity, and the monuments and inscriptions go back to the fifth century B.C. An interesting, but unfortunately fragmentary, inscription from the period of Hecatomnid control of Lycia (see above, pp. 25–6) records grants made by the dynast Pixodarus to the cities of Xanthus, Tlos, Pinara, and Cadyanda, and suggests (though the incompleteness of the text makes this only conjectural) that these cities assisted him in a campaign against the Carian city of Caunus. If so, this is the one appearance of Cadyanda in history. Coins of the city are exceedingly rare, if they exist at all; the abbreviated name may easily be misread for Calynda or Candyba. Despite its obscurity, however, the extant ruins of the city are considerable, and testify to its vigour and healthy prosperity under the Roman Empire.

Perched on its hilltop 1,300 feet above Üzümlü and nearly

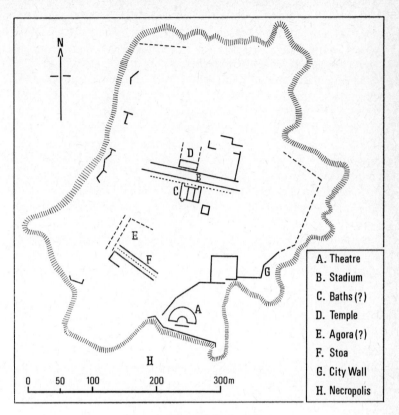

FIG. 3 Plan of Cadyanda

A. Theatre
B. Stadium
C. Baths (?)
D. Temple
E. Agora (?)
F. Stoa
G. City Wall
H. Necropolis

3,000 above the sea, Cadyanda was certainly in a commanding situation. The ancient Greeks, like the modern Turks, made light of a thousand-foot climb at the end of their day's work. The more comfortable ascent leads round the hill from the north side by the east to the south; the more direct path is very steep but convenient for the descent. On the way up is a group of four handsome tombs; three of these, of house-type, are cut in large boulders which have fallen later and are now lying at odd angles. The fourth stands free on all four sides and appears to be cut from the solid rock; the two long sides are decorated with very fine reliefs—on the south side a man reclining on a couch

(Pl. 5), on the north a mounted warrior riding over a fallen foe and charging down another who carries a shield and a spear raised ineffectually skyward (Pl. 6). These tombs are dated around 400 B.C. or a little earlier.

Approaching the site from the south the visitor comes first upon an immense number of tombs or graves, most of which have been illicitly dug in recent times and are consequently destroyed or badly damaged; a few still stand more or less intact. Some consist of a vaulted chamber originally covered with plaster, a type common at Olympus on the east coast, but not characteristic of Lycia as a whole.

A little further up is the city-wall, fairly well preserved in this part, but hardly discernible elsewhere. Just inside it is the theatre, small and in poorish preservation. Many of its seats survive on the west side, and the semicircular retaining wall of the cavea stands all round; it is built against the excavated hillside and is visible only from the interior (Pl. 7). The stage-building is a more or less unintelligible ruin.

Across the city centre, from west to east, runs a long open space some 30 feet wide and over a hundred yards in length (B on the plan; Pl. 8), not unlike the main street at Phaselis.[1] Nevertheless, despite its dimensions and its unusual position, there is no doubt that this is a stadium. The city must have possessed a stadium, as the inscriptions mention two athletic festivals celebrated at Cadyanda. Eight statue-bases of athletic victors have been found in or around it, and six rows of seats are partially preserved on the north side; along the south side runs a line of blocks. Except at the west end it is much over-grown. The original length is in fact uncertain, as the ends are destroyed, and may have approximated more nearly to the standard length of some 200 yards.

Adjoining the stadium on the south is a building (C) in ashlar masonry of the Roman period, divided into three chambers, with three large windows on the south side (Pl. 9). The western chamber has an apse at its south end. An inscription lying close by records that the emperor Vespasian built the baths out of the money recovered by him for the city. We know nothing of course of the circumstances, but it is interesting to have this

---

[1] *Turkey beyond the Maeander*, p. 163.

evidence of the interest taken by the emperor in the affairs even
of the minor cities of his empire. The building C must evidently
be the baths in question, though its form is unusual for a baths
of the Roman period. The three chambers are now in a state of
ruin, but a small building close to one corner is still standing in
fairly good condition.

Across the way on the north side are the jumbled ruins of a
large building (D) identified as a Doric temple, approached from
the stadium by steps. Little can be made of it in its present
condition and the evidence for the Doric order is not obvious;
the writer indeed noticed an Ionic column-drum lying among
the fallen blocks.

In the south-west part of the city, lost among the vegetation,
is a ruined stoa some 90 yards long (E); the space adjoining it
on the north has been dubiously identified as the agora. The
city lay too high for an aqueduct of the normal Roman type,
and a supply of water was secured by cisterns; many of these
are to be seen, half a dozen of them still containing water in
summer. The site as a whole is very attractive but much
overgrown, and to some extent spoilt by the illegal digging.

At the foot of the hill, not far from Üzümlü, are two note-
worthy tombs, though they are now sadly damaged. One stands,
or stood, near the road from Üzümlü to Ortaköy; it is a pillar-
tomb of standard type but lacking the grave-chamber at the top
(Pl. 10). It has recently been overturned and the upper stone is
cracked in two. The other stood rather less than a mile to the
south-east of Üzümlü and is, or was, among the most remarkable tombs in Lycia; it is now damaged almost beyond recogni-
tion. It was free-standing, cut from the rock, and carried reliefs
on all four sides. These included warriors, men and women
seated or reclining, and animals. On one side the male figures,
but not the female, were identified by their names in Lycian and
Greek; only one woman has a name attached, and she is called
merely 'wife of Zzala'. The tomb is dated to the late fifth
century.

LYDAE

Across the bay from Fethiye to the west is the bold headland
of Kapıdağ. On it are the ruins of Lydae, a city hardly men-

tioned in antiquity and never of much account. Its earliest
appearance is in the *Stadiasmus*, where it is called Clydae; some
two hundred years later the geographer Ptolemy calls it Chydae,
but the true form of the name is abundantly proved by the
inscriptions. For its earlier existence the only possible evidence
is a coin of the fourth century, with types resembling those of
Cnidus, inscribed with the first two letters of the name; but the
attribution is unreliable. There is no later coinage, and the ruins
themselves are exclusively of the Roman and Byzantine
periods.

The crossing from Fethiye by motor-boat takes about two
and a half hours; the trip may also be done from Göcek. There
is a tiny landing-stage at Aylimanı (or Ağalimanı) on the east
side of the headland; from here a path leads up to the ruins in
an easy half-hour's walk. The ancient city was evidently
approached by this way, as in one place the paving is well
preserved, where the rock is smoothed and crossed by transverse
grooves to prevent slipping (Pl. 11).

The site occupies most of the headland. The south end is
hilly, but the central part is hollow, with a stream, dry in
summer, running through from south to north. The path leads
to the top of the eastern slope of the hollow, and the visitor's
eye is at once caught by the ruins of two large mausolea,
originally very handsome and still in fair preservation. The
northern (Pl. 12), measuring some 32 by 28 feet, is approached
by a flight of steps now buried under débris; fragments of a
statue, Corinthian column-shafts, and other architectural
members are lying around. The entrance was on the east, but
this side is largely destroyed. Inside is a large chamber with a
low bench along three of the walls; on this sarcophagi were
apparently placed, fragments of which have been seen. Above
the bench were three large vaulted niches, two of which are
preserved. In the exterior of the north wall two doors lead into
smaller chambers under the main chamber; they were closed by
sliding panels, for which the groove is visible in the right-hand
door. Here again a bench runs round three walls.

The southern mausoleum, rather larger than the other, still
stands over 22 feet in height, but the east and north walls have
largely collapsed; the entrance is on the west, where the pivot-

hole for the door may be seen in the threshold-stone. In the
south wall are two doors leading to smaller chambers under the
main chamber. Here too many ornamental blocks are lying
around. These mausolea are not earlier than the mid-second
century.

Down in the hollow, in the city centre, is an open space
which is bounded by lines of blocks at right-angles; this is
identified as the agora. On its west border is a group of three
buildings side by side, with passages 9 or 10 feet wide between
them. Their purpose is not clear. Further to the west is a built
tomb of broad-and-narrow masonry, in good preservation. At
the south-east corner of the agora is a small building in ruins,
in front of which on the west is lying the torso of a colossal
statue in dark marble, and at its back a large base with a
dedicatory inscription. A little to the east of the agora is another
small building with the remains of eight rectilinear rows of
seats; this may possibly be some kind of council-chamber.
Across the stream to the west a Lycian sarcophagus and a badly
preserved theatre have been recorded; the present writer has
seen neither of these.

A short distance south of the city is a steep hill on which
stood a fort, almost the only defence that Lydae possessed, as
there was never a city-wall. The fort is of good solid masonry
and very irregular plan; the northern part was separately
fortified. In the interior is a large cistern. On the high ground
to the east of this fort are other walls and some house
foundations.

At the northern end of the peninsula, and separated from the
city centre, is a group of ruins identified by the inscriptions as
those of Arymaxa, a deme of Lydae. The name is otherwise
quite unknown. Not much remains apart from some Byzantine
structures and numerous tombs, some sarcophagi, some rock-
cut of pigeon-hole type. There is, however, a small fort near the
isthmus which joins the peninsula to the mainland, and a late,
or even modern, wall across the isthmus itself. A steep and
difficult path leads up from the shore below.

LISSA

If the enterprising traveller will follow the track northward from the isthmus for something over two miles, he will come in sight of a large marshy lake, the Kargın Gölü. Here, at a spot called Kızılağaç, are the scanty ruins of Lissa. The place is now deserted. Lissa is mentioned in the ancient writers only by Pliny, in the corrupt passage already discussed (see above, p. 42). It never struck coins and is identified only by inscriptions found on the spot. Nor is there very much to be seen today. The acropolis hill was defended by a wall partially preserved, of regular ashlar; in the south face of this are built the inscriptions naming the city, the surface of the blocks being smoothed to receive the writing. They are honorific decrees dated by the regnal years of Ptolemy II and Ptolemy III in the third century B.C. Otherwise nothing remains of Lissa apart from numerous tombs between the city and the sea; most of these are simple cist graves formed of stone slabs set upright in the earth. Lissa must have possessed public and private buildings like any other city; the inscriptions speak of the assembly and magistrates; the total disappearance of these on a site away from the sea, which for many centuries, and for many miles around, has been almost uninhabited, is certainly remarkable.

CHAPTER FIVE

Xanthus

OF ALL THE CITIES IN LYCIA Xanthus probably has the most romantic appeal. Although the site was previously known, it was made familiar to the Western world by Sir Charles Fellows. His first visit in 1838 so impressed him, especially with the Lycian sculptures, that he paid it a second visit two years later; the publication of his journals aroused such interest that in 1842 H.M.S. *Beacon*, accompanied by Lieutenant Spratt, was sent to bring back to the British Museum the works of art which he had discovered and recorded. For two months the sailors were busy stripping and carrying off the monuments; finally more than seventy huge cases of sculptures and inscriptions arrived in England. The contents caused almost as great a sensation as the Elgin marbles had done forty years earlier, and the Xanthian room has always been among the most popular.

The Xanthus river, now the Eşen Çay, the most considerable river in Lycia, flows close under the city on the west side, and has the distinction of being mentioned by Homer. The current is strong, flowing knee-high in August, as the writer can testify from the painful experience of fording it on foot. The name, meaning 'yellow', is one of the few Greek place-names in Lycia; the Lycian name was Sirbis or Sirmis, which has been thought to be connected with the Arabic *asmaru*, yellow or brown. The Lycian name of the city was Arñña.

Xanthus was at all times the greatest city of Lycia. Strabo expressly calls it so, and Herodotus writes almost as if Lycian and Xanthian were synonymous terms. Nothing is reliably recorded of its foundation; legendary 'eponymous' founders by name Arnus and Xanthus are mentioned by late writers, but they may, as usual, be discounted. The importance of the city

D

is matched by its ruins at Kınık, which even after their spolia-
tion for the benefit of the British Museum are still the most
impressive in Lycia. Apart from the digging by Spratt's sailors
no proper excavation was undertaken until the French carried
out a thorough campaign from 1950 onwards.

The earliest historical mention of Xanthus is in connexion
with the Persian general Harpagus' conquest of western Asia
Minor about 540 B.C. From Caria he descended into the Xanthus
valley, where he was opposed by the Lycians. These, defeated
by numbers and penned into their city (that is, Xanthus),
collected their wives, children, slaves, and property on the
acropolis and set fire to the whole, then issuing forth perished
fighting to a man. Herodotus adds that of the Lycians who in
his time called themselves Xanthians nearly all were foreigners
except for the descendants of eighty families who happened to
be out of town at the time of the disaster and so survived. If it
be asked what they were doing away from home, the answer
must surely be that they were doing just what their modern
successors do every summer: they were up at their *yayla* during
the hot weather. The names of many of the villages in the
Xanthus valley—Kınık is one—are repeated on the high ground
of the Seki plain to the north; as soon as the crops are in, most
of the inhabitants of the lower villages trek on foot or donkey
to the upper, descending again in October. The villages near
sea-level tend accordingly to be sparsely occupied during the
tourist season.

Recovery from this calamity was not long delayed, as is
shown clearly enough by the splendid monuments erected in the
city in the fifth century. Persian rule was not heavy on the
cities, and they continued happily enough till the arrival of
Alexander in 334 B.C. The Xanthians' dealings with him are a
matter of some uncertainty. The historian Appian, writing in
the second century A.D., records that they 'are said' to have
been unwilling to submit to him, and to have suffered as on the
previous occasion, 'destroying themselves in the name of
freedom'. This is not, however, confirmed by any other evidence,
and Arrian, our most respectable authority for Alexander's
campaign, also writing in the second century, observes merely
that Xanthus was surrendered to Alexander along with Pinara,

Patara, and other places. Appian's hearsay account therefore should no doubt be rejected.

While Alexander was in the region, a portent is said to have occurred. A fountain near Xanthus suddenly welled up of its own accord and threw out a bronze tablet inscribed with archaic letters announcing the overthrow of the Persian empire by the Greeks. Alexander was encouraged by this to clear the whole coast of Persians as far as Cilicia.

In the confused period following Alexander's death (see above, p. 26) Xanthus came into the hands of Antigonus. Lycia was, however, claimed by the Egyptian king, and Ptolemy I in 309 B.C. came with a fleet and took it from him by force. After this the next that we hear of the fortunes of Xanthus comes from an inscription, later erased but still just legible, on a jamb of the south gate of the city. This informs us that 'King Antiochus the Great dedicated the city to Leto, Apollo, and Artemis'. From this unusual text it is inferred that Antiochus III, engaged in 197 B.C. in taking Lycia from the Ptolemies, finding himself unable to occupy Xanthus by force, made an agreement with the citizens, who were no doubt tired of being besieged, that they should make a nominal surrender of the city to him, on condition that he should consecrate it to the national deities of Lycia, that is in effect that he should declare it free and inviolable.

This benefit, however, was not of long duration. After Antiochus' defeat at Magnesia Xanthus with the rest of Lycia was given to Rhodes. An attempted tyranny at Xanthus in the second century, which may well have had Rhodian support, was mentioned above.

During the Roman civil wars of the first century B.C. the Xanthians staged their second (if it was not their third) melodramatic holocaust. In 42 B.C. Brutus, engaged in raising forces and money for the forthcoming show-down with Octavian and Antony, came to Lycia. The Lycian League resisted him, but were defeated, and Brutus proceeded to besiege Xanthus. What followed is described in great detail by Appian. The Xanthians first employed a scorched earth policy by destroying the city's suburbs, then surrounded it with a ditch, across which they fired on the attackers. Brutus, however, managed against all expectation to fill the ditch and pen the Xanthians in their city; then, bringing up his siege-engines, he succeeded in partially destroying the walls. As the defenders still resisted, he lured them one day into making a sally, which he easily routed. The Xanthians, retreating to the city, found the gate shut against them by the guards, who feared that the enemy might get in with them, and many were killed. A little later, nevertheless, they made a second sally and set fire to the engines; this time the gate was left open, and on their return many Romans did in fact succeed in entering the city with them. While others also were trying to force an entry through the gate, the portcullis suddenly fell, either because the ropes broke or because the Xanthians cut them. The Roman intruders, thus isolated from their friends, found themselves in difficulty and finally took refuge in the temple of Sarpedon. The Romans outside meanwhile made every effort to break down the gate, but were defeated by its iron casing, and having lost their engines and ladders were in something of a quandary. With great determination, however, they improvised new ladders, while others tied iron rods to ropes and threw them up against the battlements; whenever these caught, they hauled themselves up hand over hand. Others again attempted to scale the precipice overhanging the river; many fell to their death, but some succeeded, and by these various means a fair number got into the city. These then joined their companions outside in battering the gate from within, till at last about sunset the city was captured. The Xanthians thereupon ran to their houses and slaughtered their unresisting families. Brutus, hearing the lamentations, was seized with pity; calling on his men for restraint he sent round heralds offering a truce; spurning these the Xanthians threw all their possessions on pyres previously constructed, and setting fire to them cast themselves into the flames.

Thus Appian; other writers give different details. Plutarch has a curious story that the Romans crossed the river by swimming under water, and that the defenders caught them in nets let down into the stream with bells attached to announce any capture. The present writer finds this less than credible; in his experience the Eşen Çay is not that sort of river. Plutarch

further records that after the fall of the city a woman was seen
hanging from a noose with her dead child slung from her neck,
setting fire to the house with a burning torch. Hearing of this
Brutus was moved to tears and proclaimed a reward for any of
his soldiers who saved a Lycian from destruction. Both writers
agree that a bare hundred and fifty Xanthians fell alive into
Roman hands.

Among the minor documents surviving from antiquity is a
group of letters supposed to have been exchanged between
Brutus and the Lycians; they are of very dubious authenticity.
In them he claims to have slaughtered the Xanthians without
distinction of age and to have burned their city; the Xanthians,
he says, begged for mercy, and he justifies his severity on the
ground that those who had hoped for the fruits of victory
cannot expect to escape the pains of defeat. This hardly seems
to agree with his compassionate attitude as depicted by the
historians.

Xanthus recovered again from this further disaster, with
encouragement from the emperor, and continued under the
Empire to enjoy pride of place among the Lycian cities; many
monuments were constructed, such as the arch of Vespasian, a
new theatre, and a new agora. In Byzantine times the city-walls
were renovated and a monastery built on the top of the hill. The
city had its bishop, though he ranked rather low under the
metropolitan of Myra.

The coins of Xanthus identified by name are of Hellenistic
date, though it is highly probable that many of those struck by
the dynasts before Alexander, and of those struck in the name
of Lycia under the Empire, were actually issued at Xanthus.

The old bridge over the Eşen Çay has now been replaced, none
too soon, by a modern structure which brings the visitor into
the village of Kınık at the foot of the site of Xanthus. The old
road leads up through the middle of the city and offers a
car-park by the Roman agora. Across the agora to the south is
the theatre, and beyond this the Lycian acropolis, the original
city-centre. On its flattish summit the French excavators have
laid bare a mass of foundations; these belong to a succession of
building periods, and the resulting network is not easy to

understand. The plan (Fig. 4) makes no attempt to show all the details; specialists who are interested are referred to the excavators' publications.

The acropolis was defended by a wall dating to the fifth century B.C., in polygonal masonry, which remains in part on the east, south, and west sides; the north side is wholly Byzantine and has effaced the early wall. At the north-east corner stands a pillar-tomb some 14 feet high, with the grave-chamber preserved at the top, visible from the acropolis above. It has a Lycian inscription on the north side; on the east two words survive of a Greek inscription which tells us that the pillar has been moved to this place from elsewhere; this is likely to have happened in the second century A.D. when the theatre was built or rebuilt. In general, when the vast Roman altera-

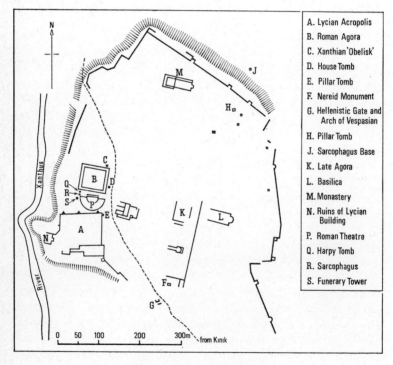

A. Lycian Acropolis
B. Roman Agora
C. Xanthian 'Obelisk'
D. House Tomb
E. Pillar Tomb
F. Nereid Monument
G. Hellenistic Gate and Arch of Vespasian
H. Pillar Tomb
J. Sarcophagus Base
K. Late Agora
L. Basilica
M. Monastery
N. Ruins of Lycian Building
P. Roman Theatre
Q. Harpy Tomb
R. Sarcophagus
S. Funerary Tower

FIG. 4 Plan of Xanthus

tions including the theatre and agora were made, care seems to
have been taken to preserve the old Lycian monuments.

In the south-east corner of the Lycian acropolis are the
foundations of a square building comprising several rooms
which is thought to have been the palace of the dynasts in the
earliest times, destroyed at the time of the capture by Harpagus.
It was replaced by another building of which the basement
survives; the upper parts were apparently of wood. This was
destroyed by fire in the fifth century and was not replaced.
Higher up to the west is a small sanctuary with three parallel
chambers, and on the highest point, just to the west of a large
cistern, are the scanty remains of a temple of the Lycian
equivalent of the Greek Artemis. At the west extremity stood
a building which must originally have been very handsome; its
architecture seems to have imitated the wooden houses whose
features appear also in the tombs of house-type, and was
decorated with a sculptured frieze; the blocks of this frieze were
re-used by the Byzantines for repair of the acropolis wall, and
were later removed to London by Fellows. Just to the north-
west of this building is a rectangular foundation on which stood
a pillar with a pediment on two sides; this too has gone into the
Byzantine wall.

Most of the north-eastern part of the acropolis is occupied by
an extensive monastery. This includes a church set against the
east acropolis wall, and to the west of this an open courtyard
with wash-basins along one side. The other foundations round
about belong to the various rooms of the monastery.

Backed against the massive Byzantine wall of the acropolis
is the theatre. As it stands this was built in the mid-second
century A.D.; a handsome donation of 30,000 denarii by
Opramoas of Rhodiapolis was earmarked specifically 'for the
construction of the theatre'. If there was an earlier theatre on
the site, it has been totally obliterated by the Roman. The rows
of seats are well preserved, but were originally much more
numerous; several rows at the bottom were removed when a
wall was built around the orchestra, and many more at the top
were lifted and re-used in the Byzantine wall. The orchestra is
at present full of blocks from the stage-building; this had the
usual columned façade in two storeys forming the background

of the stage, of which the front wall is standing in part. The orchestra is entered on the east by a parodos leading through an arch; the corresponding parodos on the west is a mere dummy for appearance's sake and does not lead through to the outside.

Just above the theatre on the west are two conspicuous Lycian monuments excellently preserved (Pl. 14). That on the north is the famous Harpy Tomb, so called since Fellows's time through a dubious interpretation of its reliefs. The massive base has been recently cleared by the excavators; the pillar itself, with the grave-chamber and crowning slabs, stands 25 feet high. Large square lifting-bosses have been left projecting on three sides. The chamber at the top was of marble and decorated with reliefs; these were removed by Fellows and the covering stones propped up by wooden struts and a pile of stones. In this mutilated condition the tomb remained till 1957, when the Turkish authorities installed the cement casts which have done much to restore the beauty of the monument. The reliefs are interesting, but, as often, not easy to understand. On all four sides are seated figures receiving gifts, on the south and east sides a bird, on the north a helmet; on the west side are two seated females, that on the right approached by three standing figures, the other receiving an indistinct object. On the east side are three other female figures, that on the right apparently accompanied by a dog. The figures which have given the tomb its name are on the north and south sides on either side of the seated figures; they represent bird-women with female heads, wings, and tails, carrying children in their arms. When the tomb was first discovered, these were recognized as Harpies carrying off the daughters of Pandareos, as described by Homer: the children were left orphaned and were befriended by Hera, Athena, Artemis, and Aphrodite; when Aphrodite went to Olympus to arrange a suitable marriage for them, leaving them unprotected, the Harpies came and snatched them away to be servants to the Furies. That Pandarus was a Lycian hero seemed to give support to this interpretation. But there are difficulties. Pandarus and Pandareos are two different heroes; the latter had two daughters, not four; and the children on the relief are obviously not of marriageable age. More recently scholars have preferred to see in the winged females the other bird-women of mythology, the Sirens, carrying the souls of the dead, in the form of children, to the Isles of the Blessed. The seated figures are then members of the dynastic family; formerly Hera and Aphrodite were recognized on the west side, and Artemis with her hound on the east. All the reliefs were originally coloured, chiefly in red and blue, traces of which were visible at the time of the discovery. On the back of the relief-slabs were painted crosses and other symbols, suggesting that at some time the grave-chamber was used as a refuge by some Christian anchorite.

The other monument, just to the south of the Harpy Tomb, is also sepulchral but of totally different type. It consists in fact of two tombs, a sarcophagus of normal Lycian type standing on a stunted pillar-tomb. The latter is not monolithic but constructed of slabs set upright leaving a space in the interior. This space was used for the burial, which was found intact and dated by the pottery to the third century B.C.; it included, however, a relief-slab, now in Istanbul, representing funeral games and dating from the sixth century. This must apparently have belonged originally to another pillar-tomb. The sarcophagus also, therefore, must be no older than the Hellenistic period, unless we may suppose that it too has been taken from elsewhere and re-employed. The monument as a whole is most unusual, indeed virtually unique.

A third monument, a little further to the south, has the form of a tower containing a funeral chamber; it is thought to date from early Imperial times.

Two other sepulchral monuments stand beside the Roman agora. On its east side, between the agora and the road, is a free-standing house-tomb on a remarkably massive substructure (Pl. 16); at its east foot is the entrance to the basement chamber or hyposorium.

The other, at the north-east angle of the agora, is the famous Xanthian Obelisk (Pl. 15). 'Obelisk' is not in fact a good name for it, as it is simply a pillar-tomb of perfectly normal type. The upper part has suffered a good deal of damage, but many of the fragments have been recovered by the excavators; they show that the tomb possessed the usual grave-chamber, enclosed like the Harpy Tomb by slabs with reliefs showing the dead man, surely one of the dynasts, victorious over his enemies. The topmost block of the roof bears marks of the feet of a statue, no doubt the dynast himself. But the fame of the monument derives from the inscription which covers all four faces of the stone; it is the longest Lycian inscription known, running to over 250 lines. Linguistically it falls into three parts; beginning on the south side it continues on the east and part of the north side in the normal Lycian language; then follows a poem of twelve lines in Greek; but the rest of the north side and the whole of the west is couched in that strange form of Lycian which appears elsewhere only on a tomb at Antiphellus (see below, p. 96; above, p. 22).

As was said above, the Lycian language is little understood apart from the frequently repeated epitaphic formulae; the present inscription, on the other hand, evidently gives a narrative account of the dead hero's exploits, and is still undeciphered. It does, however, contain a number of recogniz-able proper names, from which the approximate date and some idea of the contents may be gathered. The hero in question is called, in the Lycian and in the Greek, son of Harpagus (not of course the Persian general of the sixth century); his own name is lost in both places, but he appears to be the Xanthian dynast, known from the coins, who appears several times elsewhere in the inscription in the Lycian form KERẼI. In the Greek epigram he is said to have been a champion wrestler in his youth, to have sacked many cities, slain seven Arcadian hoplites in a day, set up more trophies than any other man, and added glory to the family of Karikas. This Karikas appears as KERIGA seven times in the Lycian; he too is known from the coins as a Xanthian dynast. Both he and KERẼI are dated to the latter part of the fifth century B.C. And to this same period belong the historical names recognizable in the Lycian. In addition to Athenians and Spartans, Darius and Artaxerxes, we have more especially a mention of the Athenian Melesandrus (MILASÃÑTRA) who was sent to Lycia in 430–429 B.C. to collect tribute and prevent the Spartans from intercepting the Athenian cornships. He failed and was killed in battle. It is likely that his defeat was among the exploits of KERẼI.

The extensive area across the road to the east of the agora is the inhabited quarter of the Hellenistic and Roman city. It has not been excavated, except for the Basilica (L on the plan) of which the foundations have been laid bare, including many blocks re-used from the Lycian city. But on the eastern edge of this area, close inside the city-wall, are a number of Lycian tombs, more or less damaged, which have, or had, handsome reliefs. Pl. 17 shows a sarcophagus lid with the representation of a boar-hunt; Fig. 5 shows another with an unusual scene. Two horsemen are galloping to the right; the hinder, from whatever cause, is in the act of falling from his mount. On the left is an armed warrior, at a higher level and on a much smaller scale. It has been thought that he is the victor, presumably the owner of the tomb, the others the vanquished fleeing from him, one of them wounded. But it is curious that he is shown so small, and with his head turned away; and the alternative suggestion is made that the owner of the tomb is the falling man, killed simply by a fall from his horse, while the figure on the left shows him in his normal state. Deaths from accident are not uncommonly recorded on tombstones.

Fig. 5 Xanthus. Sarcophagus Lid

Further to the north in this region stood the sarcophagus of Payava, one of the finest at Xanthus; little of it remains on the spot, the splendid reliefs having been removed to London. Close by, however, near the east foot of the acropolis hill, is a particularly picturesque group of tombs (Pl. 18). It is dominated by a pillar-tomb in excellent preservation; the grave-chamber at the top is of white marble, without decoration. The entrance is on the south side. In the rocks below is a series of tombs, mostly of Lycian house-type; one, however (not shown on Pl. 18), is in Greek style, with a porch in the Ionic order and epistyle and pediment above. Its inscription, on the other hand, is in Lycian.

Beyond the city-wall to the north and east is a multitude of tombs, rock-cut and sarcophagi; among the most attractive is that shown on Pl. 19, with a fine relief of two lions mauling a bull. On the summit of the hill, the Hellenistic and Roman acropolis, all that is to be seen is a fairly well preserved monastery of Byzantine date which is likely to have replaced a Roman temple.

At the lower end of the city, just above the village, the road passes under the site of the well-known Nereid Monument, an exceptionally richly decorated tomb dating to the fifth century B.C. Only some of the architectural members remain, all the sculptures having been taken to the British Museum. Directly across the road is the south gate of the Hellenistic city, largely destroyed but carrying the inscription recording the consecration of Xanthus by Antiochus III; and close behind this is a Roman archway still standing, dedicated to the emperor Vespasian (A.D. 69–79) by the Council and People of Xanthus (Pl. 20). The pavement which survives in part belongs to an ancient road which led up from Patara and the Letoum.

THE LETOUM

Across the river from Xanthus, $2\frac{1}{2}$ miles to the south-west and 2 miles from the coast, is the well-known sanctuary of Leto. Until 1962 little was to be seen beyond a theatre and a mass of blocks marking the site of a temple; since then the French excavators have uncovered the major part of the sanctuary and adjoining buildings, working largely under the water-table, and have recovered many interesting documents concerning it. The excavation is continuing at the time of writing, and the publication is not yet complete.

The story of Leto commonly current in antiquity related that she was loved by Zeus, thus incurring the hatred of Hera. Persecuted by that jealous and unforgiving wife, she was sent to wander from place to place until she finally arrived on Delos and there gave birth to Apollo and Artemis. Among the countries visited by her during her wanderings some accounts included Lycia; there, it was said, she approached a certain fountain to relieve her thirst, but was driven away by the local herdsmen who wished to water their own cattle. Later, after her children were born, she came back to Lycia and punished the herdsmen by turning them into frogs. One account adds that when driven from the fountain, she was guided by wolves to the river Xanthus to assuage her thirst, and in memory of this changed the country's name from Termilis to Lycia.[1] And there was even a local legend that Apollo and Artemis were actually born in Lycia (see below, p. 71). Yet another story was that Leto was befriended in Lycia by an old woman named Syessa who received her into her hut. Some have thought that the cult of Leto may have been established in Lycia even before the Greek period, and that her name may be connected with the Lycian LADA, 'woman' or 'wife'.

Other shrines of Leto are known not far away to the north-west, near Calynda and Physcus, but they have not the celebrity of the Xanthian. Leto and her children were the national deities of Lycia, and the Letoum was the federal sanctuary of the Lycian League. National festivals were celebrated there, and its priests were the chief priests of the League. The ruins, as now revealed by the excavators, confirm the size and importance of the sanctuary.

The centre of the site is occupied by three temples side by side (Pl. 21); none is preserved much above floor-level. Closest to the rocky ledge on the east is a Doric temple with a peristyle of eleven columns on the sides and six at the ends, dating to the latter half of the second century B.C. It had the normal pronaos,

[1] *Lykos* is the Greek word for wolf.

cella, and opisthodomus; the cella walls were adorned with engaged half-columns. Furthest to the west is a somewhat larger temple in the Ionic order, apparently slightly earlier in date. It is also rather better preserved, and the fragments allow a reconstruction in large part. It too had a peristyle of eleven columns by six, and engaged half-columns in the cella walls. Between these two is a smaller and much earlier building, which surprisingly included a rocky outcrop in its northern part. It is identified by a Lycian dedication to Artemis (ERTEMIT) of the fifth or fourth century. For the identification of the other two temples there is no specific evidence, but they are supposed to be respectively of Leto and Apollo.

To the south and west of the main temple (of Apollo?) excavation has revealed a large nymphaeum connected with the sacred spring (Pl. 23). A rectangular building oriented east–west is bordered by a large semicircular paved basin, and flanked on the north by two semicircular exedrae. It dates to the third century A.D. and replaces an earlier Hellenistic building. The excavation was conducted largely under water, and the greater part is now permanently flooded. Part of the nymphaeum was later overlaid by a church, dating apparently to the sixth century.

A Hellenistic stoa to the north of the temples, another to the west, and other buildings are in process of excavation at the time of writing. Remains of the Lycian period are more deeply buried, but sherds have come to light which go back to the eighth century B.C.

To the north of the precinct is a large and well-preserved theatre of Hellenistic date. The cavea, which faces north-west, is more than a semicircle and in its middle part is cut out of the hillside; the ends are built of regular smooth-faced ashlar. There is one diazoma. A vaulted passage leads to the cavea on either side; that on the south-west has on its inner face a row of sixteen masks, representing among others Dionysus, Silenus, a satyr, a girl, and a comic old woman. No sign of a stage-building is visible. Close above the north-east entrance is a fine tomb; the door, which is half buried, is narrow, with leaf decoration at the top corners. The interior is spacious, of very large, beautifully cut squared blocks. Between this and the entrance to the theatre is a 30-foot stretch of early polygonal wall, with blocks measuring up to 5 feet.

Among the inscriptions recovered by the excavators is a remarkable trilingual text in Lycian, Greek, and Aramaic, found below the rock-shelf to the east of the temples. The three texts refer to the establishment at Xanthus of a cult of the Caunian deity Basileus (King). This was a deification of the mythical founder, Caunus son of Miletus; his cult, under the title of 'King', was observed at Caunus down to Roman times,[2] and is now attested in the fourth century B.C. during the satrapy of Pixodarus, brother and successor of Mausolus. The inscription provides for monthly and annual sacrifices; offenders against the regulations shall be guilty before Leto, her children, and the Nymphs.

Mention may also be made of the curious stone figure shown on Plate 22. The present writer found it in 1946 lying on top of a thorn hedge. It is 3 feet high, neither statue nor bust, being cut off just above the legs. Most attention has been given to the face; the ears and arms are mere shapeless lumps; the back is flat. The figure seems clearly to be unfinished, and is perhaps a pupil's discarded exercise. The stone was removed to Fethiye and set up in a garden; what happened to it after the earthquake of 1957 the writer cannot say.

Strabo places the Letoum ten stades (rather over a mile) from the river-mouth and sixty stades from Xanthus. The former figure may be correct, as the coastline is likely to have shifted since antiquity; the sixty stades to Xanthus, on the other hand, cannot be reconciled with the facts and must be an error.

An easy hour's walk to the west is a small site which appears to be that called variously in the ancient authorities Pydnae or Cydna; it is now known as Gâvur Ağlı ('Infidels' steading'). It is no more than a fort, consisting merely of a ring-wall enclosing an area of some four acres, but the state of preservation is so good that it serves as a model of ancient fortification. The wall, slightly over 3 feet in thickness, is in beautiful polygonal masonry, the blocks modestly bossed and fitted with superb accuracy (Pl. 24). There are two gates, one at the east corner,

[2] See *Turkey beyond the Maeander*, p. 169.

one at the north, and eleven towers unevenly spaced. On top of the wall are laid flat slabs, projecting strongly on the inside; in the sloping parts they give the appearance of a stairway. On them a breastwork of rubble and mortar has been erected, but this is evidently a much later addition. In seven places steps lead up to the wall. The towers, still up to twenty courses or over 30 feet high, have a door on the inner side; they were in two storeys, the upper giving onto the ramparts, and cornices in the inner face show where the floorboards of the upper storey were laid across. In the east corner are the ruins of a church. Fellows in 1840 saw a broken base carrying a vow to Poseidon; this has not been seen again, nor has anything else ever been found in the interior, and the writer in 1946 was no more fortunate.

1 Daedala. Roadside tomb.　　2 Telmessus. Tomb of Amyntas.　　3 Telmessus. Tombs beside the Tomb of Amyntas.

5 Cadyanda. Tomb on hillside.

4 Telmessus. Lycian sarcophagus.

6 Cadyanda. Tomb on hillside; north face.

7 Cadyanda. Theatre.

9 Cadyanda. Building beside the stadium.

8 Cadyanda. Stadium.

11 Lydae. Ancient roadway.

10 Cadyanda. The fallen Pillar-tomb.

12 Lydae. Mausoleum.

13 [*opposite*] Xanthus. Site from the Acropolis hill.

14 [*opposite*] Xanthus. Sarcophagus and 'Harpy Tomb'.

15 Xanthus. The 'Obelisk'.

16 [*opposite*] Xanthus. Tomb beside the Agora.

17 [*opposite*] Xanthus. Carved sarcophagus lid.

20 Xanthus. Gate of Vespasian.

19 Xanthus. Tomb on Acropolis hill.

18 Xanthus. Tombs on Acropolis hill.

22 Letoum. Curious carved figure.

21 Letoum. The newly excavated Temples.

23 Letoum. Nymphaeum.

24 [*opposite*] Gâvur Ağlı.

25 [*opposite*] Tlos. Citadel and Agora.

26 Tlos. Roman building beside the Agora.

27 Arsada. Horseman deity.

28

29

30 Araxa. Post-Lycian tomb.

28 [*overleaf*] Araxa. Acropolis wall.

29 [*overleaf*] Araxa. Group of tombs west of the village.

CHAPTER SIX

The Xanthus Valley I

TLOS

Tlos, 9 miles from Kemer, is now easily reachable by a tolerable, though rutted, road; the acropolis is directly above the village of Yakaköy. The neighbouring village of Düver is also frequently given as the site of Tlos. It is conspicuous by a Turkish castle on top of the hill, in which Spratt in 1842 was entertained by the brother of the Ağa; it is now unoccupied.

Of the high antiquity of Tlos there can be no doubt. In the Lycian inscriptions the name appears in the form Tlawa, and Hittite records of the fourteenth century refer to a city of Dalawa in the Lukka lands; the identity is virtually certain. The classical city of Tlos, though numbered among the six principal cities of Lycia possessing three votes in the League, is never mentioned by any ancient writer apart from a mere note of the name in the geographers. Its history is confined to two incidents recorded in the inscriptions. The help given by Tlos and other Lycian cities to the dynast Pixodarus in the fourth century B.C. was mentioned above (p. 42), as also was the attempted tyranny by a certain Eudemus in the second century, probably with Rhodian backing (see above, p. 27). Inscriptions tell us further that the citizens were divided into demes; at least three are known by name, called after the famous Lycian heroes Bellerophon, Iobates, and Sarpedon. A Jewish community is also mentioned, with its own magistrates. Under the Empire Tlos bore the title of 'very brilliant metropolis of the Lycian nation', and in Byzantine times it had its own bishop under the metropolitan of Myra.

The site of Tlos was discovered in 1838 by Sir Charles Fellows, who thought it 'splendid and appropriate'; Spratt, who

E

followed him, observed that 'a grander site for a great city could scarcely have been selected in all Lycia'—high praise in a country abounding in grandeur. The acropolis hill is not high, at least on the side facing the town, but ends on the north-east in almost perpendicular cliffs. The summit is now occupied by the castle, which has obliterated anything earlier. Below it on the east slope are traces of the Lycian city-wall and below that a long stretch of a subsequent city-wall; the latter at its south end is of respectable Roman masonry, with a gate, but at the north end it is constructed with much re-used material, including column-drums and a broken sarcophagus. On the same slope are two picturesque groups of Lycian tombs, one just below the summit, the other towards the north end.

At the foot of the hill on the east is a large flat open space now cultivated, which has been thought to be the agora; many column-stumps and other carved blocks lie round its edges. Down the middle run lines of blocks forming an elongated oblong; this appears to be original, but its purpose is not clear. Along the west side, below the city-wall, are rows of seats in the hillside, partially visible in the photograph (Pl. 25). These belonged to a stadium, of which the other side is now marked by a low wall, or rather a line of stones, which is not original. The level to which the seats descended is shown by a line of carved blocks still *in situ*; beside this runs a stream, which has apparently disrupted the original installation. Such a position for the agora, running alongside the stadium, would be unique in the writer's experience.

The opposite, east, side of the open space is flanked by a long building, over 30 feet wide, not divided into chambers, with half a dozen small rectangular doors in its west wall, presumably a market-building. At the south end of this is a wider building with several chambers and four large arched doors; then after another building are another four arched doors, and further on another four (Pl. 26). Beyond the south end of this complex, a little to the east, is a baths, of which there still stand two complete rooms and an apsidal projection with seven windows, called locally Yedi Kapı, the seven doors. East of this the corners of a large open piazza have recently been identified, with the suggestion that this, rather than the open space described above, was the agora. West of the piazza is a large Early Byzantine church.

Further to the east is the theatre, large and in very good preservation, but at present wretchedly overgrown. The date of its construction is known with unusual precision; among the benefactions of the philanthropist Opramoas of Rhodiapolis in the time of Antoninus Pius (A.D. 138–161) was a gift of 60,000 denarii 'for the construction of the theatre and of the exedra in the Baths'. The baths in question is presumably that described above. An inscription also records donations for the building of the theatre from private citizens, ranging from 3,000 drachmae by the priest of Dionysus and high priest of the Cabiri to more modest contributions of 100 drachmae.[1] The whole theatre stands on flat ground, with a semicircular cavea, in the Roman manner, and there is evidence that it was planned, and perhaps begun, a century or more earlier. Thirty-four rows of seats have been counted, though it is not easy to count them today; there is a single diazoma, approached, on the south side at least, by an arched entrance. A corridor runs round the outside of the cavea. Much of the stage-building survives, overgrown like the rest, with many finely carved and decorated blocks. This handsome theatre is crying out to be excavated, or at least cleared.

Of the numerous tombs cut in the face of the acropolis hill the largest and most remarkable is the so-called Tomb of Bellerophon, low down on the north side. This is of the temple-type, with two square pilasters between antae and pediment above. Inside the porch the front wall of the tomb proper is divided into three parts: in the middle an imitation door with studs and other ornamentation, and on either side a real door leading to a grave-chamber. These side-doors are raised over three feet from the ground by threshold blocks, each of which carries on its front a relief representing a horse.[2] Above the left door is an animal facing left, apparently a lion or leopard, and on the upper part of the left wall of the porch, facing right, is Bellerophon mounted on Pegasus with his right arm raised behind him (Fig. 6). The suggestion which at once comes to

[1] The Greek drachma was equated with the Roman denarius.
[2] Formerly thought to be dogs.

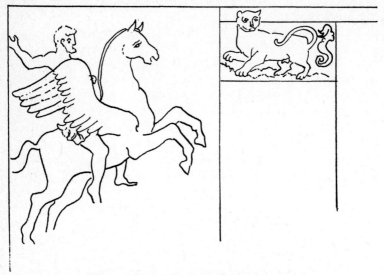

FIG. 6 Tlos. The Bellerophon Tomb

mind is that it was intended to show Bellerophon attacking the
Chimaera, as in the familiar story; but the scale of the two
figures is different, nor has the animal the traditional features
of the Chimaera.[3]

Inside the left-hand door is a funeral chamber with four stone
benches for the dead; one of these, on the right side, has a
pillow for the dead man's head and a niche for offerings; this
is no doubt where the head of the family was laid. The right-
hand door leads to a smaller chamber with three benches. The
tomb carries no inscription, so that the owner's name is
unknown; it has, of course, never been supposed that
Bellerophon himself was buried here.

ARSADA

Arsada lies somewhat back from, and high above, the Xanthus
valley, on an upland plain on the side of Akdağ, the ancient Mt
Massicytus. The altitude is over 3,000 feet. There is no road, and

[3] See the illustration in *Turkey's Southern Shore*, p. 169.

the site must be approached by a long and steep path from Kayadibi. Arsada is not mentioned by any author in antiquity, but the identity is proved by an honorific decree of the Arsadans found on the spot, and by the evident survival of the name in the village of Arsaköy close by.

Just to the west of the village is a long low hill, precipitous on the west towards the valley, and bearing on its east slope, about half-way up, a wall of dry rubble about 8 feet thick; a stretch of some 300 yards is preserved, but in poor condition. At its north end this wall runs up to a tower or small fort 30 feet square, constructed of large polygonal blocks carefully laid; it seems to date to the early Hellenistic age.

Of the town itself none of the buildings remain, but in and around the village are a number of Lycian tombs, mostly of 'Gothic' sarcophagus type, one of which has human heads represented on each of its short sides; but most of them are now overthrown. There is at least one rock-tomb of house-type, and many sculptured and inscribed blocks are lying around. The inscriptions are almost all epitaphs. Spratt reported having

Fig. 7 *Ex-voto* Dedication to Kakasbos

noticed three imperfect Lycian inscriptions, but of these nothing has ever been seen since.

A little above the village, beside the path from the north, on an outcrop of rock about 8 feet high, is a relief representing a horse and rider (Pl. 27). The horse is prancing to the right, the rider's right hand is raised behind him and carries an elongated object of uncertain character, and he seems to have had a sword slung over his left shoulder. This looks like one of the Anatolian horseman-deities; the best known of these is Kakasbos, who appears frequently in western and northern Lycia; but he is excluded here, since he never carries a sword but always a club and his horse always proceeds at a gentle walk.[4] We should naturally suppose an *ex-voto* dedication, but there is no inscription to identify the deity.

ARAXA

Araxa is situated by the village of Ören at the upper, northern end of the Xanthus valley, close under the mountains. It is identified by several inscriptions naming the city. Though it is listed by the ancient geographers, nothing further was known of it until the present writer found at Ören in 1946 a long decree of the people of Araxa recording the public services of a distinguished citizen by name Orthagoras. The stone was then in use by the women of the village as a washing-board, for which the lines of writing provided an admirable surface. From it we learn that in the second century B.C. Araxa was involved in wars first with Bubon, then with Cibyra, whose men had ravaged Araxan territory and carried off a number of its citizens; Orthagoras was sent as ambassador to complain to the League. At the time of the attempted tyrannies at Tlos and Xanthus he served with distinction in the League army until the usurpers were suppressed, and again in a war between the Lycians and Termessus. He was instrumental in obtaining the admission to the League of a neighbour of Araxa called Orloanda, a place otherwise unknown, and later functioned as ambassador to meet certain envoys from Rome. In all these cases he served without pay and secured whatever was needful for his city.

[4] A characteristic representation of Kakasbos is shown on Fig. 7.

Not much now survives of Araxa. In the village are the ruins
of a massive building, of which one wall, making an obtuse
angle, stands to a height of 10 feet; the masonry is polygonal
approaching the regular in places, the blocks well fitted. On the
acropolis hill, which is quite low, a little below the summit on
the side towards the village, are the remains of a solid wall
(Pl. 28) with a tower projecting 18 feet; the blocks are huge,
measuring up to 5 feet 10 inches by 5 feet 5 inches, laid in nearly
regular courses; many of them have drafted edges.

Down by the riverside are lying numerous 'Gothic' sarcophagus lids with illegible inscriptions, but the most interesting
tombs are in a group of a dozen cut in the rock at the base of a
low hillock by the roadside about a mile to the west of the
village. They are of various types; most are of true Lycian
house-type, one group of three being especially attractive
(Pl. 29), others are plain rock-cut chambers. One, however, is of
different and later form (Pl. 30); the porch is flanked by two
antae, each decorated with two rosettes in front and one on each
side, with capitals of no particular order; above is an architrave
with two fasciae, a dentil frieze, a slight cornice, and a naked
pediment lacking the normal raking cornices. A tall door leads
to the usual chamber with three benches. Above the main group
is a plain Lycian tomb with the name Orthagoras carved on
either side of the door. This is the only inscription in the group,
but it is not original; it relates to a re-use of the tomb in much
later, apparently Roman, times, and the man in question is not
to be identified with the Araxan hero mentioned above.

Not far from Ören towards the mountains is an unusually
abundant spring, which issues from the ground and immediately
forms a deep and strong stream; this joins the main course of
the Xanthus near the village and very greatly increases its
volume and strength. But recent water-works on an extensive
scale have altered the state of things in later years. There was a
local legend in ancient times that Leto gave birth to Apollo and
Artemis not on Delos but in Lycia; the poet writes that the
river Xanthus was revealed to men by her, when 'in the bitter
pangs of her divine labour she tore up with her hands the hard
soil of Lycia'. An inscription found at Sidyma localizes the birth
precisely at Araxa. The remarkable spring just mentioned is

today commonly regarded by the local inhabitants as the source of the Xanthus, and the visitor may, if he wishes, picture the many jets of water released by Leto's tormented fingers as she scored the ground in her agony.

CHAPTER SEVEN

The Xanthus Valley II

PINARA

The Carian poet Panyasis, a kinsman of Herodotus in the fifth century B.C., wrote that Tremiles, who lived by the river Xanthus, fathered four sons, Tloos, Xanthus, Pinarus, and Cragus, thus inaugurating the Lycian nation. This 'eponymous' founder of Pinara is as unsubstantial as the rest. Another story was told by the Xanthian historian Menecrates in the fourth century to the effect that the Xanthians, suffering from overpopulation, 'divided their elders into three groups, one of which went to Mt Cragus and founded a city on a round peak and called it Pinara, which being interpreted means "round"; for the Lycians called all round things *pinara*'. Whatever credence this story may deserve, the explanation of the name seems likely enough to anyone who has seen the remarkable circular crag which towers above the ruins. In actual fact the Lycian name in the inscriptions is not Pinara but Pinale; the interchange of liquids is of course common enough.

There was perhaps a Pinaran at Troy. Homer tells of the Lycian archer Pandarus who fought in the Trojan army, and we learn from Strabo that there was a cult of Pandarus at Pinara. Mention was made above of the inscription recording help given by several Lycian cities, including Pinara, to the Carian Pixodarus. In the later historians the only reference to the city is in connexion with Alexander's conquest of Lycia in the winter of 334–333 B.C., and this merely records that he accepted its surrender. Despite this lack of a history there is no doubt that Pinara ranked among the foremost cities of Lycia; Strabo indeed says as much, and Stephanus calls her a 'very great city'. And the extant ruins go far to justify this estimate. She certainly possessed the maximum of three votes in the League assembly. A dozen inscriptions in the Lycian language have been found on the site, but they are all epitaphs on rock-tombs and tell us nothing beyond the names of the occupiers; and the Greek inscriptions are little more informative. The known coins are all of the second or first century B.C. Later, when Opramoas was distributing his hand-outs to the Lycian cities, Pinara was not forgotten; she received 5,000 denarii for the repair of her public buildings.

The name Pinara has survived, assimilated to the Turkish word for a minaret, in the village of Minare half an hour below the ruins. The village is easily accessible by a short road, recently constructed, branching off the main Fethiye–Xanthus road. As he climbs from the village, the visitor's eye is first caught by the great round mass of rock which seems to have given Pinara its name. It rises some 1,500 feet above the city below, ringed by perpendicular cliffs and accessible only by a difficult path on the south side. This path was barred at the top by a triple wall, which survives in part, but elsewhere a wall would be superfluous. On the broad, flat sloping surface of this crag the earliest city of Pinara was founded; only slight traces of it remain, notably cisterns and smoothed rock-foundations for houses of wood and mud-brick. The summit, on the south-west, carries a fort defended by walls and a ditch; but this, like the sherds of tiles and vessels, dates apparently to occupation of the hill in medieval times. But the most striking thing about this hill is its vertical east face, which is honeycombed with hundreds of rectangular pigeon-hole tombs (Pl. 31), quite inaccessible without tackle. They are arranged in two horizontal groups, with a blank strip between, and were evidently cut with the use of ladders from below and ropes from above. They date no doubt to the city's earliest days.

This original acropolis cannot have sufficed for long, and its place was taken by a much lower hill rising out of the valley at its east foot. On and around this are extensive ruins of the classical city. They are largely lost among rocks and vegetation, and a thorough exploration requires considerable time and effort; the villagers, however, will readily conduct the visitor to the principal showpieces. This lower city was never defended by

a wall; presumably the old acropolis served as a refuge in time
of need.

Between the two acropolis hills are numerous unidentifiable
ruins and many tombs, mostly sarcophagi; one of these, towards
the south end, is of unusual size, certainly among the largest in
Lycia. Other sarcophagi are set around it in a square, the whole
forming a striking group (G on the plan). Just to the south of
this are two rock-cut house-tombs, and close by are the remains
of a Christian church. In the west face of the lower acropolis,
near the north end, is a small theatre or odeum, but it is in
wretched condition, utterly overthrown and overgrown.

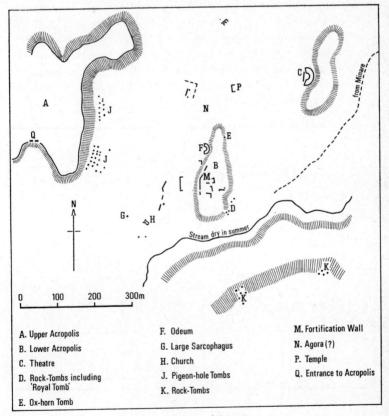

FIG. 8 Plan of Pinara

A. Upper Acropolis	F. Odeum	M. Fortification Wall
B. Lower Acropolis	G. Large Sarcophagus	N. Agora (?)
C. Theatre	H. Church	P. Temple
D. Rock-Tombs including 'Royal Tomb'	J. Pigeon-hole Tombs	Q. Entrance to Acropolis
E. Ox-horn Tomb	K. Rock-Tombs	

On the other, east, side of the hill, low down, is an exceptionally fine rock-tomb of house-type which has been dubbed the Royal Tomb (D on the plan; Pl. 32). The door-lintel carries a band of relief showing many people and horses; the scene is not easy to understand, but seems to be peaceful. Above this is a row of square beam-ends forming a kind of dentil frieze; two of them have masks sculptured on their front ends. Above again is a pediment with another scene in relief, but it is too much broken away to be readily intelligible. Fellows, in whose time more may have been visible, thought to see in the pediment group the instruction of a child, and on the lintel a group of persons rejoicing. The interior of the porch is unusually interesting, as it has on its side-walls, right and left, representations of four walled cities, one of which is shown in Fig. 9. All four are generally similar and show battlements with gates, towers, houses, and tombs; in three of them human figures are visible, one of whom seems to be a watcher at the gate, the others are standing in peaceable attitudes. Some observers have

Fig. 9 Pinara. Relief in Porch of the 'Royal Tomb'

thought to discern certain resemblances to the cities of Xanthus
and Telmessus, but they are far from exact and can certainly
not be pressed. Fellows even thought that all four together
represented Pinara itself, but this cannot be right, if only
because Pinara was not a walled city. In any case the reliefs on
this tomb have nothing of the warlike character which is so
common on others. The interior consists of a single chamber
with one bench at the back, raised unusually high above the
floor. This, and the great size and decoration of the tomb,
suggest that it is the burial-place of a single person, surely a
prince, though there is no inscription to identify him. The
building has unfortunately suffered a great deal from wanton
damage and from the fires lit inside it by the peasants. A few
yards to the south is a most attractive group of tombs cut in a
lofty angle of rock (Pl. 33).

At the south end of the lower acropolis is a splendidly
preserved specimen of a house-tomb, and much higher up, in the
east face towards the north, is another interesting tomb. This
too is of house-type, but its roof is in the form of a Gothic arch,
and at the point of the arch is a pair of ox's horns. This last
feature is very rare, if not unique; the horns have no doubt an
apotropaic purpose, to scare away the evil-intentioned, much
like the horses' skulls which are so commonly used as scarecrows
or at the gates of the fields in Turkey today (Pl. 34).

Below the north end of the hill is an area of level ground
which is likely to have been the agora, though little or nothing
survives to identify it. On its east side are the scanty remains
of a temple, a large foundation some 45 by 27 feet, and other
remnants of buildings now quite unidentifiable. About a
hundred yards to the east is another low hill, in the west face
of which is the main theatre, in very good preservation and
recently cleared. The cavea is virtually complete, forming more
than a semicircle, with 27 rows of seats and ten stairways
making nine cunei; there is no diazoma. The plan of the stage-
building is quite clear, and parts of its walls and pillars are still
standing to a height of 5 or 6 feet. Two doors are preserved at
the south end, and still had their lintels in place until recently;
both lead into the space between the proscenium wall and the
main building, one from the parodos, the other from the side of

the building. The proscenium wall bends back at each end at an obtuse angle to run parallel with the analemma and so form a parodos with parallel sides. The theatre as a whole is purely Greek, and seems never to have been Romanized.

In the extreme south of the site, in the hillside beyond the stream, are more rock-tombs, handsome and well deserving of a visit, though requiring something of an effort to reach.

SIDYMA

Sidyma is, apart from Arsada, the least often visited of the cities of the Xanthus valley. It is indeed, like Arsada, hardly to be reckoned in the valley at all, being situated high up on Mt Cragus, 1,750 feet above the sea, and quite inaccessible to wheeled traffic. From the main Fethiye–Xanthus road a side-road turns off 6 kilometres south of Kestep (Eşen); this may be followed by a jeep for another 6 kilometres, after which there is a fairly steep 800-foot climb of an hour or so by a good, if stony, path. A guide is essential.

The form of the name Sidyma (like Idyma, Didyma, and Loryma) is proof enough of a high antiquity for the city. There is in fact some evidence on the site itself for occupation at least in the early classical period; but the first literary reference is not before the first century B.C., and the bulk of the ruins, and all the inscriptions, are of the Roman Imperial age. There exists, however, a silver coin of Lycian League type, apparently of Sidyma,[1] which dates probably to the second century B.C. The city continues to be listed by the geographers down to Byzantine times, but only a single incident is recorded of her history. The emperor Marcian (A.D. 450–457), at the time a simple soldier on a campaign against the Persians, fell sick on the way through Lycia and was left behind in Sidyma. There he was befriended by two brothers who took him into their home and nursed him; and one day, when he was recovered, they took him hunting with them. At midday, hot and tired, they lay down to sleep. One of the brothers, waking before his companions, was astonished to see that Marcian was sleeping in the

[1] It carries the abbreviation SI, which can hardly be other than Sidyma; the alternative, Simena, is unlikely to have struck coins.

sun and that an enormous eagle had settled on him and was shading him with its outstretched wings. When all were awake, the brothers asked Marcian, 'If you become emperor, what favour will you do us?' Marcian replied, 'In that unlikely event I will make you Fathers of your city'. When he did in fact succeed to the purple on the death of Theodosius II, he remembered his promise and, going one better, appointed the brothers to high office in Lycia.

As the visitor climbs the path from the east described above, the first indication of the ancient city is a large number of open pigeon-hole tombs cut in the cliff on the left hand. They are reminiscent of those at Pinara, though much less numerous and impressive; how old they may be is uncertain. On reaching the top of the path the ruins of Sidyma are at once in view, and the visitor finds himself among a group of tombs of varying designs quite well preserved. The most interesting, though not the most spectacular, is a small pillar-tomb just above the path on the left. It consists of a single tall rectangular block set on a rectangular base; the grave-chamber at the top is missing (Pl. 35). This is the first piece of material evidence for Sidyma's existence in the classical period.

Close by is a group of seven tombs. Some of these are sarcophagi, notable for having gable-shaped lids instead of the normal Lycian 'Gothic' shape. Others are built tombs, one of which, shown on Pl. 36, is particularly handsome and well preserved.

The main site is on a level plain, a mile or more long, running north-east and south-west. The village of Dodurga (Asar Mahalle) has changed its position since the last century and is now in the middle of the ruins; this has caused damage to the city centre, and not all of the buildings previously described can now be made out. The acropolis hill, in two parts, lies on the north; along its south-east foot runs a stretch of early wall some 400 yards long and still 10 or 12 feet high in places. The masonry is mostly regular ashlar, but polygonal at the east end (Pl. 37), and at one point is a small gate with a forecourt and flanking tower. This wall provides the second piece of material evidence for an early city of Sidyma, set on the hill above.

Remarkably enough, no trace of this early city has survived on the hill; there are some walls, cisterns, and sherds, but they are all of the Byzantine age. There is, however, a little above the early wall a small theatre or theatre-like building, very badly preserved; when the writer saw it, six rows of seats were partially visible at the back, but anything else which may have survived was buried under the earth and stones that have slipped down the hillside. This theatre belongs of course to the later city.

The city centre, which is also the village centre, lies at the west end of the site. Here there were formerly to be seen remains of a temple and stoa sufficient to permit a reconstruction on paper. The back wall of the stoa is still recognizable, with a public convenience set against it, but not much of the temple can now be made out. It was quite small, about 30 feet in length, with steps and four columns on the west front, and was dedicated 'to the Saviour Gods the Emperors'. Part of the inscription of the stoa also was found, with a dedication to the emperor Claudius (A.D. 41–54), Artemis, and other deities.

Between here and the east end of the site are numerous monuments, mostly tombs. The most striking is shown on Pl. 38. It is a built tomb of temple-type, raised on two steps, and seems originally to have had two columns in antis, though these are no longer to be seen. A large slab of the roof remains in place, decorated on the underside with soffits containing human heads and rosettes in relief. The heads are beardless and appear to be female. At the rear a plain opening leads to a lower chamber.

Close by is a row of sarcophagi, two of which especially catch the eye (Pl. 39). They are identical in form and size and rest on a common base. Like the others at Sidyma they have a gable-shaped roof, with acroteria at the lower corners. The badly weathered inscriptions show that, as would be expected, the two tombs belong to members of the same family, apparently father and son, both bearing the name Aristodemus, which seems to have been regularly repeated in the family. One inscription shows the occupant to have been a court physician honoured by the emperors; the other is in verse, the initial letters of the lines forming an acrostic, Aristodemus.

A short distance to the south-west is a conspicuous building still standing 30 feet high (Pl. 40). It rests on a low substructure which originally formed the base of a large built tomb, but the building itself is of much later date and contains many re-used blocks, some inscribed. There are windows high up in the walls. The door on the north side is decorated with lions' heads on the lintel and a rosette at the top of each jamb. A low door in the rear wall of the substructure led to the basement of the original tomb.

Mention may also be made of a building further to the west which may perhaps have been a baths, though little of it remains apart from two arches side by side. There are many other ruins on the site, including those of two churches, but they will not detain the ordinary visitor for long.

In the village a mosque has recently been constructed, largely out of the stones of Sidyma; let into its back wall is an unusual inscription headed 'The Gods here', followed by a list of twelve deities. The names are all familiar, Zeus, Apollo, Artemis, Athena, Aphrodite, and so forth, but surprisingly two deities named in other inscriptions, Hecate and Serapis, are not included. The Twelve Gods of Lycia are well known,[2] but they are anonymous; was the present list perhaps restricted to twelve in order to give them names? It is not to be supposed that all twelve possessed temples at Sidyma; in fact the only temple yet identified on the site is dedicated to the Emperors.

[2] See *Turkey's Southern Shore*, p. 43, Fig. 2.

F

CHAPTER EIGHT

Patara

A STORY WAS TOLD that a certain Spanish girl was carrying from Greece to Lycia a box containing sacrificial cakes in the shapes of lyres, bows, and arrows, intended as offerings to Apollo. On the way she rested by the sea-shore with the box at her side, and while she slept, a strong wind blew the box into the sea. On waking to find it gone she returned home in tears; but the box was carried by wind and waves to the shore of Lycia. There it was found by a countryman of hers who duly made the sacrifice. The story is told by a Greek writer of the first century B.C., and the word used for the box is *patara*; from this the city of Patara received its name. Now the word *patara* is not Greek, nor yet Lycian, but is apparently the same as the Latin *patera*, a plain indication that the tale is a comparatively late invention.

Other legends relate to much earlier times. The usual 'eponymous' founder is again in evidence, by name Patarus; he is made to be the son of Apollo and a nymph Lycia. Another version makes him son of Lapeon and brother of Xanthus, though Xanthus is elsewhere called son of Tremiles; and in yet a third account the son of Apollo and Lycia who founded Patara is called Icadius. The utter confusion and unreliability of these myths could hardly be clearer. It is surprising that so respectable an author as Strabo should accept, or at least quote, the foundation by Patarus.

More interesting is the evidence connecting Patara with Telephus, a hero of the time of the Trojan War. Telephus was wounded by Achilles, and was told by an oracle that the wound could only be healed by the wounder; this was eventually done by means of the rust from Achilles' spear. Which god gave the oracle is not stated, but there is convincing evidence that it was

Apollo at Patara. Pausanias says that the Lycians exhibited in the temple of Apollo at Patara a bronze bowl which they claimed to be an offering by Telephus and the work of Hephaestus; and at Lindus on Rhodes there was once a golden dish inscribed: 'Telephus to Athena, by command of the Lycian Apollo'. Moreover, there is said to have been, less than a mile from Patara, a Spring of Telephus; the turbidity of its water was explained by the hero having bathed his wound there. There was also a deme of Telephus, presumably at Patara, though it is not mentioned in the inscriptions.

In truth Patara was a Lycian foundation. Its Lycian name, known from coins and inscriptions, was PTTARA, which has been compared with the Chaldaean *ptari*, a town. Surprisingly, not a single Lycian inscription has been found on the site itself.

The temple and oracle of Apollo at Patara had a high reputation in antiquity, and are said to have been in early times comparable to Delphi itself in riches and the reliability of the oracle, though apart from the legendary case of Telephus no actual response of Apollo is recorded. Herodotus says that the prophetess, when there is one, is shut in the temple at night; for, he adds, the oracle at Patara does not function all the time. In fact it was understood that Apollo regularly spent the six winter months at Patara and the six summer months on Delos. With regard to the form of the temple and the method of divination we have no information, unless we may infer from Herodotus that the god's response was revealed through the dreams and visions of the priestess. Among the conflicting accounts of the original foundation of the oracle the most picturesque alleges that Danaus, king of Argos, was told by Apollo to go forth until he found a wolf and a bull fighting each other, and to mark the outcome; if the bull was victorious, to build a temple to Poseidon, but if the wolf came off best, to dedicate a shrine to Apollo. In the event the wolf was the winner, and Danaus built a temple to the Lycian Apollo.[1]

The history of the oracle was not uninterrupted, and for a period about the beginning of the Empire it seems to have fallen into complete disuse. Mela, writing in the first century under Claudius, speaks of it as having *formerly* rivalled Delphi.

[1] *Lykos* is the Greek for a wolf.

This decay, and a subsequent revival in the second century, is attested by the inscription recording Opramoas' benefactions under Antoninus Pius; among other gifts to the Patarans he presented 20,000 denarii 'to the account of their ancestral god Apollo, whose oracle, after a long period of silence, has now again begun to prophesy'. That Servius in his commentary on the *Aeneid* should speak of the oracle in the past tense is not of course significant, for he was writing soon after the famous edict of Theodosius in A.D. 385 which put an end to all oracles.[2] Surprisingly, no trace of the temple or oracle has yet been discovered on the ground.

As the principal port on the coast of Lycia, Patara had a long history. Alexander in 333 B.C., after accepting its surrender, offered it to the Athenian general Phocion as one of four cities from which to choose the revenues; this, says the historian, was a noble offer, but Phocion displayed even greater nobility by declining it. During the wars of Alexander's successors Patara enjoyed considerable importance as a naval base, in which capacity it was occupied by Antigonus in 315 B.C. and by Demetrius at the time of his siege of Rhodes in 304. In the third century the city came with the rest of Lycia under Egyptian control; Strabo reports that Ptolemy II 'restored' it (from what, we do not hear) and changed its name to Arsinoe in honour of his sister-wife; but the old name soon revived. In 196 B.C. it fell to Antiochus III of Syria (see above, p. 26) and was held by him, despite repeated efforts by the Romans and Rhodians to capture it, until the treaty of Apamea in 189 B.C. (see above, p. 26) compelled him to relinquish all his possessions in these parts. In the following year a number of his ships which were still at Patara were burnt by order of the Roman consul. In 88 B.C. during the first Mithridatic War the king laid siege to Patara for a time, and committed the offence of cutting timber for his siege-engines in the Letoum, till a dream persuaded him to desist.

In 42 B.C., after the disaster at Xanthus, Brutus proceeded to Patara, where he offered the choice of submission or a similar fate. The Patarans at first resisted, though the Xanthians implored them to have more sense; Brutus gave them the rest

[2] See *Aegean Turkey*, p. 238.

of the day to reflect, and the next morning they decided to submit. According to Plutarch this change of heart was brought about by certain female prisoners whom Brutus, fearing a repetition of the Xanthian horror, released without ransom in the hope that they would induce their fathers and husbands to surrender the city. This they duly did by representing Brutus as the most reasonable and honest of men. Dio Cassius, however, has another version. According to this the release of the female prisoners did not have the desired effect; Brutus therefore set up a slave-market in a safe place outside the walls and proceeded to sell the male captives one by one. When this was equally ineffective, after selling a few he set the rest free. Then at last the Patarans were convinced that he was a good man and submitted without more ado. The historians agree that Brutus punished the Patarans neither with death nor with exile, but merely ordered that all gold and silver, public or private, in the city should be handed over. Money was after all the main object of Brutus' campaign in Lycia.

Under the Empire Patara maintained her status as one of the principal cities of Lycia, not only by her possession of three votes in the Lycian League, but also as the seat of the Roman provincial governor and the repository of the League's archives. These last were probably kept in the temple of Apollo. The city further enjoyed the title of metropolis, and in the fourth century acquired high honour in Christian circles as the birthplace of Nicholas, bishop of Myra.

The harbour of Patara, the most important in Lycia, which made Patara, in Appian's words, 'as it were the port of Xanthus', is now no more. In its place is an extent of open ground, marshy in winter and in places also in summer, nearly a mile long from north to south and about a quarter of a mile wide, cut off from the sea by a broad sand-dune. Parts of it are now under crops. The site is known as Kelemiş, but there is no village and the place is virtually deserted. The harbour seems to have been surrounded in antiquity by a wall, of which there are some scanty remains, especially on the east side. From the ancient accounts of Brutus' dealings with the Patarans it appears that the city as a whole was fortified, but of any such

defence wall no trace is now to be seen. The city's buildings,
public and private, were simply grouped around the edges of the
harbour. The whole site is flat, apart from a hill some 130 feet
high at the south end, at the entrance to the harbour on the
east.

The ruins are reached by a tolerable road branching off the
road from Xanthus to Kaş. As the visitor approaches by this
way he comes first to a handsome triple-arched gateway
standing virtually complete (Pl. 42). It is of the familiar Roman
type. Beside the arches on either face of the gateway are six
consoles which formerly carried busts identified by their
inscriptions, which still remain, as those of Mettius Modestus,
governor of Lycia-Pamphylia about A.D. 100, and members of
his family; the building is accordingly dated to this time.
Another inscription on the north face records its construction by
'the People of Patara, metropolis of the Lycian nation'. Just to
the west of this gate is a slight eminence which has produced
good-quality Attic pottery of the classical period; it has been
suspected that this may be the site of the long-lost temple of
Apollo, but here, as elsewhere at Patara, no proper excavation
has been done.

Close to the south foot of this mound are the ruins of a
building (B on the plan) which consisted of two side-chambers
connected by a vaulted roof; this has been variously understood
as a baths or as an edifice intended for shipbuilding. The state
of preservation is poor. The basilica C is also unspectacular.
Much more attractive is the small temple K a little to the west,
though it needs to be cleared of the vegetation. It dates from
the second century A.D., and has a single chamber with a door
over 20 feet high and very rich decoration laid on in stucco; the
order is Corinthian. According to the custodian this building is
now commonly known as the temple of Apollo, presumably
because it is the only temple yet identified on the site; it is in
fact much too small and simple for so famous a building, even
if it be regarded as a late successor to the original temple.

To the south of the basilica is a better-preserved baths, built
according to its inscription, 'together with its swimming-pools
and additional decoration', by the emperor Vespasian (A.D.
69–79) out of funds kept for the purpose and a sum of money

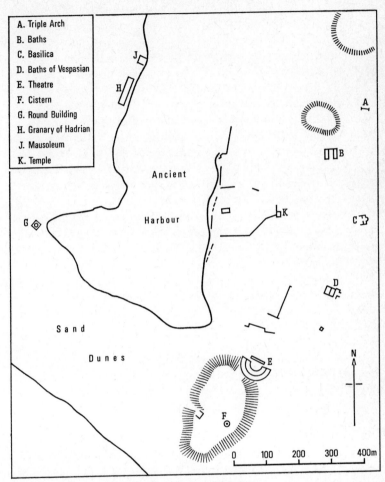

A. Triple Arch
B. Baths
C. Basilica
D. Baths of Vespasian
E. Theatre
F. Cistern
G. Round Building
H. Granary of Hadrian
J. Mausoleum
K. Temple

FIG. 10 Plan of Patara

contributed by the League. It comprises five chambers joined
by doors; these correspond evidently to the apodyterium or
changing-room, the frigidarium, the tepidarium, the caldarium,
and the sudatorium,[3] though nothing is now visible to identify
them. Two small chambers at the east end may have held the
furnace. The multitudinous holes in the walls are nail-holes for

[3] See *Aegean Turkey*, p. 229.

fixing a veneer of marble or bronze; that this was a later
addition is shown by the fact that the holes even pierce the
inscription.

Further on, at the north-east foot of the hill, is the theatre
(Pll. 43, 44). This is in fact remarkably well preserved, but the
cavea is largely filled with drifting sand and the stage-building
buried in trees. Earlier visitors, who saw it less encumbered,
counted thirty-four rows of seats and measured the orchestra at
about a hundred feet. There is one diazoma. The lower storey
of the stage-building has the usual five doors to the stage and
five windows; the upper storey was pierced by arched windows.
An inscription on the outer wall of the stage-building records
that a certain Vilia Procula, a citizen of Patara, in A.D. 147
dedicated to the emperor Antoninus Pius, to the city of Patara,
and to its ancestral gods the proscenium which her father built
and the stage, with its statues and marble revetting, which she
contributed herself; while the eleventh row of seats in the upper
block and the awning over the auditorium were previously
dedicated by her and her father. But the theatre as a whole is
certainly older than this, as another inscription mentions its
repair in the time of Tiberius (A.D. 14–37) by one Polyperchon,
prophet of Apollo.

The hill above the theatre is hardly deserving of the name of
acropolis. It is quite undefended, and carries only some in-
significant traces of buildings and a few tombs. At the top,
however, is a curious construction which has aroused much
speculation (Pl. 45). It has the form of a circular pit some
30 feet in diameter and nearly as much in depth; in the middle
rises a square pillar of masonry, while a steep flight of rock-cut
stairs, with a hairpin bend, leads to the bottom. The sides of the
pit are rock-cut in their lower parts; above this the gaps in the
rock are filled with small stones fitted with mortar. The pillar
in the middle, which at present rises 6 feet above the ground,
is constructed of well-cut squared blocks, three to a course,
which are still in perfect condition for the lowest nine courses;
the part above this is less well constructed, the sides are rather
shorter, and the whole is twisted out of place. Various views
have been held as to the purpose of this pit. The most absurd
suggestion is that it represents the oracle of Apollo; even if its

form should be considered suitable, it is clear from Herodotus that the oracle was in or attached to the temple. A more attractive theory is that it was a lighthouse; placed over the entrance to the harbour, its situation seems at first sight appropriate. But on the spot the attraction vanishes; the pit is not on the summit, but below it on the side away from the sea; and why should it be sunk so deeply into the ground? In the present writer's opinion the original suggestion made by Gell in 1810 is unquestionably correct, namely that we have a cistern. Its present condition indicates two periods of construction; at first a simple rock-cut cistern up to the level of the ninth course of the pillar, later enlarged by adding the masonry in the sides and by raising the height of the pillar. The stairway is no doubt original. The purpose of the pillar was to facilitate roofing against the summer heat, at first presumably with horizontal slabs; later it was built up to its present height to afford a sloping roof.[4] A cistern of this kind would be highly desirable at Patara in early times, as the site is almost entirely devoid of running water. (Visitors should go supplied!) Later the city was fed by aqueducts, of which more will be said below; much later again, perhaps when these had fallen into decay, the cistern received its additions and came into service once more.

On the western side of the harbour mouth is another interesting building which has been supposed with much greater probability to be a lighthouse. Only the foundations have survived, and these, regrettably, have become covered by the drifting sand, so that very little can now be seen. Formerly a rectangular stepped base was visible, on which lay the collapsed ruins of a circular building also raised on steps. Some blocks of its inscription have been found, each carrying a few letters, but unfortunately the only complete word that can be recovered is 'constructed'. Holes in the grooves of the letters show that these were filled with strips of bronze. The lighthouse, if such it was, stood probably on a mole at the entrance to the harbour, long since buried under the sand.

Further to the north is the Granary of Hadrian, identified by a Latin inscription running along the façade, and still standing

---

[4] A similar cistern and pillar, on a much smaller scale, may be seen on the acropolis at Pergamum.

complete apart from its roof. Here again the vegetation is a tiresome impediment. Over 200 feet long and 80 feet wide, the building is divided by cross-walls into eight rooms of equal size, originally vaulted, connected with each other by doors set close to the front wall. The façade is in two storeys divided by a cornice, below which eight rectangular doors lead to the individual rooms; above each door is a window in the upper storey. The interior, on the other hand, seems to have had only a single storey. Above each door in the façade is a pair of consoles which presumably carried busts, as in the case of the triple gateway A.

Close to the granary on the north are the ruins of a built tomb which must once have been very handsome. It was in temple form, approached by steps on the harbour side, with four columns in front. One wall is still standing, adorned by half-columns on its outer face and still carrying one course of the vaulted roof with its coffered panels (Pl. 46). Of the door only half of one upright is standing. The blocks of the wall on the inside have projecting rims along the horizontal edges; these were left during the building to avoid damage to the edges of the blocks, and should have been cut away, but for some reason this was never done. There are numerous other tombs, including some sarcophagi with rounded lid and crest.

Drinking-water must have been a problem at Patara in early times; as was said above, it is virtually non-existent on the site. In Roman times it was supplied by aqueducts, of which fragments of two are still in evidence, one on the west and one on the east. Beyond the Xanthus river, near Özlen, is a short stretch of a normal Roman aqueduct in polygonal masonry; this may have served Xanthus rather than Patara. The other is about 5 miles east of Patara, in the hills above Kalkan, and is of less normal type. A dip in the ground is crossed by a wall 20 feet high and a quarter of a mile long, also in polygonal masonry with large blocks; it is entered by two narrow doors. The water-channel ran above, consisting in the usual way of squared blocks pierced through the middle. That this led to Patara is beyond doubt, though nothing of it remains in the vicinity of the city.

For pre-Roman times there is no sign of a water-supply on the site apart from the one cistern on the theatre hill. This by itself would certainly be totally inadequate for a city. In its present condition, if rendered watertight, its maximum capacity would be about 140,000 gallons. Allowing a gallon per person per day, and allowing further for replenishment by rain during the winter, this might furnish fresh water for some 800 persons. The population of Patara in the Hellenistic period would hardly be less than ten times this figure (see below, Appendix). And at that time the cistern was smaller than it is now. The rest must have come from wells; the harbour-water was certainly not drinkable, and the only alternative would be the Xanthus river at a distance of 4 miles.

CHAPTER NINE

Central Lycia I

PHELLUS AND ANTIPHELLUS

THE SITE OF ANTIPHELLUS at Kaş has always been known; until quite recently the town was called Andifli, and this name is still frequently heard. In the last century the administrative centre of the district was at Kaş Kasaba to the north; when it was transferred to Andifli, the name Kaş went with it, and the name Kasaba remains for the former capital, now reduced to the status of a village. The site of Phellus, on the other hand, has been disputed, and will be discussed below.

The situation of Antiphellus is one of the most striking on the Turkish coast. The town of Kaş is placed on the neck of a small peninsula running out to the west, with a narrow landlocked bay between it and the main coastline; the ruins extend around the town and across the isthmus. But the whole scene is dominated by the great vertical cliff which towers over it to a height of 1,500 feet and gives the place its impressive character. The road from the north makes its way obliquely down this cliff, and another path leads up to the high ground on the west. The road to Xanthus, recently constructed, keeps along the shore; it is still rather rough, but passable for a private car with reasonable caution.

Phellus and Antiphellus are among the few Lycian cities which have a Greek name. The Greek word *phellos* means 'stony land',[1] which is appropriate enough in central Lycia. The name is at least as early as the fourth century B.C., since a bilingual epitaph found at Kaş describes the dead man in Greek as an Antiphellite; previously, according to Pliny, the place was called Habesos. At the same time we find on coins and

[1] Its other meaning, 'cork-oak', seems less appropriate.

inscriptions of the time of the Lycian dynasts a name Vehinda in connexion with Antiphellus; it occurs, for example, in the Lycian part of the bilingual inscription just mentioned. In 1952 excavators sank trial pits in numerous places at Kaş; the almost totally negative results showed clearly that in the fourth century Antiphellus was a very small place indeed, consisting of little more than a few buildings around the harbour and a number of rock-tombs. There can be no doubt that at that time Antiphellus was merely the port of Phellus. Vehinda will then be the Lycian name of Phellus, together with its port of Habesos, the Greek and Lycian names co-existing so long as the Lycian language remained in use.

In Hellenistic times the situation changed. Commercial

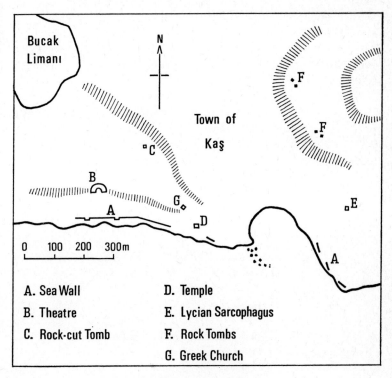

FIG. 11 Plan of Antiphellus

interests became predominant, and Antiphellus rose rapidly in importance, with a corresponding decline of the mother-city Phellus. By the time of the Roman Empire Antiphellus was the leading city of the region. Trade was no doubt largely in timber from the Lycian forests, but the only product of which we actually hear is sponges; Pliny reports that the softest were found around the walls of Antiphellus. The city issued coins in the Hellenistic age, both federal (that is, of League types) and non-federal, then, as usual in Lycia, not again until Gordian III (A.D. 238–244).

The harbour of Antiphellus, like that of Kaş, lay on the seaward side of the isthmus. Here a reef runs out to sea, providing some protection; it may have been artificially strengthened in ancient times, but even with modern improvements the harbour is suitable only for small boats. The coasting steamer anchors outside. The long narrow bay on the other side, known as Bucak Limanı (formerly Vathy), attractive though it looks on the map, is, as the *Mediterranean Pilot* observes, 'unsuitable for sailing vessels. North-north-easterly winds blow with great force off the mountains'. It is used today for the loading of timber, which is floated out from the shore.

Despite its vulnerable situation Antiphellus had neither an acropolis nor a city-wall. All that exists in the way of fortification is a stretch of sea-wall along the shore; to the west of the town this wall stands to a height of six courses for a length, interrupted in places, of over 500 yards. The masonry is a good regular bossed ashlar, likely to be of Hellenistic date.

From the harbour a path leads up to the west and very soon brings the visitor to the ruins of a small temple on the left (Pl. 49). Only the lower parts are preserved, to a maximum height of five courses, in more or less regular ashlar; the blocks are slightly bossed and in some cases have drafted edges. A vertical line, clearly distinguishable on the east side, where the blocks do not overlap, shows that the retaining wall was later extended or repaired. The original building is dated to the first century B.C., the extension probably to the late third century. The temple consisted of a single chamber; an excavation on its south side produced nothing significant, and it is not known to what deity it was dedicated.

The path continues westward towards the theatre (Pl. 47). This is small but practically complete and undamaged, standing to its full height. The retaining wall of the cavea, making rather more than a semicircle, is of a very irregular, but not unattractive, ashlar masonry; the blocks vary greatly in size and shape, and many of them have drafted edges. The cavea has twenty-six rows of seats, well preserved; there is no diazoma. The theatre seems never to have possessed a permanent stage-building of stone; the rough curved wall now in evidence was built out from the orchestra in recent years by the local inhabitants to provide a floor for wrestling matches.

A few minutes' walk over the hill from the theatre leads to a remarkable rock-tomb on the hillside (c on the plan). It is known as the Doric Tomb, and its form is unique (Pl. 48). Cut from the living rock in the shape of a slightly tapering cube some 15 feet high and wide, with a passage all round, it stands complete apart from some damage at the top. There is a moulding at the base and a shallow pilaster at each corner; all the capitals but one are lost. On the south side a band with mutules is preserved. The entrance, originally closed by a sliding door, has a moulded frame surrounding an aperture 6 feet high. The interior, smelly and defiled by the smoke of the peasants' fires, consists of a single chamber; the bench at the back is decorated with a frieze of small dancing figures holding hands, seventeen on the bench itself and four on each return, and floral designs at the sides. The tomb dates probably to the fourth century B.C.

In the hillside to the north of the town are a number of rock-tombs, some at least quite easily accessible. One of these is interesting as having an upper storey of Gothic-arch form and a Lycian inscription to which has been added, centuries later, another in Latin when the tomb was re-used by a certain Claudia Recepta.

Most of the tombs at Antiphellus, as elsewhere, are sarcophagi. Spratt in 1842 counted over a hundred, but the majority of these have been destroyed by the local inhabitants, who use the flat sides as building-stones; the curved lids, being less useful for this purpose, may often be seen lying alone. One, however, is remarkable both for its elegant form and its

excellent preservation (Pl. 50). It stands at the upper end of the
Postane Sokağı and consists of three parts. The hyposorium is
about 5 feet high, with a sunken floor; the door is broken open.
Above this is a plain base some 30 inches in height, these two
parts being cut from the solid rock. On top is the sarcophagus
itself, cut from a separate stone, with Gothic lid and crest; from
each side of the lid project two lions' heads resting on the paws.
The short end of the lid is divided into four panels; in the upper
two are standing figures in relief. On the hyposorium is the long
Lycian inscription, hard to read, which was mentioned above in
connexion with the Xanthian Obelisk as being couched in a
peculiar form of the Lycian language, perhaps poetical. That it
is an epitaph is sufficiently proved by the form of the monument, but the familiar funerary formulae are absent, and nearly
all the words are foreign to the normal run of Lycian epitaphs.
Needless to say, it has not been interpreted.

The city of Phellus is first mentioned by the geographer
Hecataeus about 500 B.C., though by a curious error he places
it in Pamphylia. The boundary of Lycia and Pamphylia was
never very precisely defined—Phaselis, for example, was sometimes reckoned as Pamphylian—but no reasonable arrangement
could extend it so far west as the very centre of Lycia. The
Lycian name of Phellus, as was said above, was almost
certainly Vehinda. Under its Greek name it is listed by most of
the later geographers; its coinage is Hellenistic of federal type,
and of Gordian III.

In 1842 Spratt visited an ancient city site on the mountain
of Felendağı just above the village of Çukurbağ, and from the
resemblance of the name and the situation close to Antiphellus
conjectured that it must be Phellus. Fellows two years earlier
seems to have had the same idea, but his account is very
imprecise. This view held the field until 1892, when Benndorf
expressed a preference for a much smaller site on the coast at
Bayındır Limanı, across the bay from Kaş. He relied on two
arguments, the position opposite Antiphellus and an epitaph on
the site in which the fine for violation of the tomb is made
payable to Phellus. In the present writer's opinion this is
misconceived, and the old identification unquestionably
correct. Neither of Benndorf's arguments is cogent. The prefix

32 Pinara. The 'Royal Tomb'.

31 Pinara. Cliff with pigeon-hole tombs.

33 Pinara. Tombs near the 'Royal Tomb'.

34 Pinara. Tomb with ox-horns.

35 Sidyma. Lycian pillar-tomb.

36 Sidyma. Lycian tomb.

38 Sidyma. Lycian tomb.

37 Sidyma. Early wall.

39 Sidyma. Pair of sarcophagi

40 Sidyma. Building erected on tomb-foundation.

41 Patara. Looking north from the Theatre Hill.

42 Patara. Monumental gateway.

44 Patara. Theatre.

43 Patara. The sand-filled Theatre.

46 Patara. Mausoleum.

45 Patara. Cistern on Theatre Hill.

48 Antiphellus. Tomb on the hillside.

47 Antiphellus. Theatre.

50 Antiphellus. Lycian sarcophagus.

49 Antiphellus. Temple.

51 Phellus. Sculptured tomb.

52 Aperlae. City wall.

53 Apollonia. Ornamented tomb.

54 Çindam. Lycian tomb.

55 Cyaneae. Sarcophagus.

56 [*opposite*] Cyaneae. Sarcophagus and pillar.

57 [*opposite*] Cyaneae. Lycian tombs.

59 Cyaneae. Ionic tomb.

58 Cyaneae. Lycian tombs.

anti- should not mean merely 'geographically opposite', without some political connexion; and tombs with fine payable to Phellus, many of them stated to be tombs of Phellites, are found in at least eight other places to the north and east. At Felendağı the only two legible Greek epitaphs are both of Phellites. Furthermore, a situation on the coast is unsatisfactory. Strabo and Ptolemy expressly locate Phellus inland, and significantly the *Stadiasmus*, listing the places along the coast, mentions Antiphellus but not Phellus. Pliny's notice, 'Antiphellus, formerly Habesos, and in [a] recess Phellus', is hardly helpful. If Antiphellus, as was argued above, was the port of Phellus, both cities can hardly have been on the sea. Bayındır Limanı is in fact a better harbour than Kaş, and there seems no reason for the existence of Antiphellus except to serve as a port for a city on the high ground to the north. But the most conclusive argument is perhaps the relative size and position of the two sites. That on Felendağı is at least three times the size of the other, and is in a dominating position over the wide plain of Çukurbağ; it has also an excellent water-supply. At Bayındır Limanı there is no arable territory beyond a few fields, and no drinking-water at all. Felendağı is in fact the only site in central Lycia east of Seyret which has running water.

Çukurbağ is reached by a roughish side-road from the plain of Avullu; there is then a climb of some 900 feet in something under an hour by a circuitous path to the ruins. The direct ascent of the mountainside is shorter, but is not recommended even to the young and active. The city occupies a long narrow area on the crest of the hill, some 600 yards in length and less than 200 in width. The first indication of it on the way up is a group of four sarcophagi in a row, with a fifth now fallen. A little above this, several stretches of the north wall of the city are standing, in massive polygonal masonry of early date; on the south side the wall is almost entirely destroyed down to ground-level, though its line is recognizable in places. The highest point is occupied by an enclosure with a rough wall surrounding a hollow now filled with scrub; this apparently represents a medieval fortification of the summit. The ancient monuments consist mostly of tombs, some of them very fine. Towards the west end is a free-standing tomb of house-type cut

entirely from the rock; it contains a single chamber with
benches on three sides, that at the back hollowed out. Two
fragments of a Lycian epitaph were found close by. Just to the
east of this is a curious and interesting complex, comprising a
house-tomb with two chambers, outer and inner, in good
preservation, other small tombs of various kinds more or less
broken, a semicircular wall of late masonry, and a rock-wall
carrying a relief of a huge bull a good deal damaged.

Below the city-wall on the south side is a very handsome
sarcophagus still largely uninjured (Pl. 51). It stands on a solid
base and has reliefs on three sides. On the long south side is a
man reclining on a couch holding a cup, with a figure standing
on either side of him; in front of him is a table, and below the
couch are two birds resembling pheasants. On the short west end
is a man, apparently a warrior, but partly destroyed by a large
hole broken into the tomb, and on the lid above two facing
griffins in the two panels; on the other short end is a man
standing with arms outstretched, while a smaller figure on the
left hands him a helmet. There are a number of rock-cut Lycian
tombs on the south slope of the hill, some partly buried; one at
least has a Greek inscription of the Roman period.

Alone among the cities of the region, that on Felendağı is very
well supplied with water. There is a rich spring on the east slope
of the hill, and a fountain in the village of Çukurbağ; not far
away, at Pınarbaşı, is a particularly abundant spring which
today supplies Kaş. And on the hilltop, inside the city-walls,
two wells have recently been sunk; the water is good and very
cold.

A very different picture is presented by the site at Bayındır
Limanı. The harbour is small but good; according to the
Mediterranean Pilot, 'the port is easy to enter and affords good
shelter. Vessels either anchor or moor with hawsers to the
shore'. It is used on occasion today. In the cliff-face above the
harbour on the left is a small group of rock-cut tombs, one of
which has a Lycian inscription. A breakneck path leads up the
cliff to the site above; the writer found it actually dangerous,
and a slip is likely to be fatal. There is, however, another way
up at the back. That the ruins represent an ancient city need
not be doubted, but it was very small, hardly more than

200 yards in length. The wall, in fair preservation, is of mixed masonry; in one place it is of a very neat polygonal, standing well over a man's height. At the upper end is a small fort, also of polygonal masonry. Inside the wall practically nothing survives except a broken sarcophagus. Outside the wall are several sarcophagi, one of which bears the inscription assigning the fine for violation to Phellus; the fine is unusually large, no less than 10,000 drachmae. The date is about the second century B.C. Arable land is almost non-existent, and communications with the interior are very poor.

The name of this city seems to be determinable. A Greek writer of the first century B.C. records a harbour of Lycia by the name of Sebeda. Until quite recently Bayındır Limanı was known as Port Sevedo, which surely preserves the ancient name. The city above the harbour had naturally the same name. Sebeda is never mentioned elsewhere, and its obscurity agrees well with the very modest dimensions of the site.

On the high ground to the west of Kaş there are a number of ancient sites, though none of any great size. The most considerable is above the *yayla* of Seyret, overlooking a long valley down which a stream runs to join the Felen river. The site, about 2,400 feet above the sea, occupies three small hilltops and has a wall of unbossed polygonal masonry of apparently early date; the whole is comparable in extent with the site at Bayındır Limanı. At one point a gate 8 feet high stands isolated, and seemingly not in the line of the city-wall. Inside are many remains of buildings and houses with doors still upright, rock-cuttings, and at least half a dozen Gothic sarcophagi with fallen lids. At the foot of the hill on the north is a pillar-tomb standing on a vaulted substructure roofed with large slabs, which appears to be the actual grave-chamber. Close by are several rock-tombs, one with a Lycian inscription. It has been suggested with good probability that this site represents the 'village of the Seroiateis' mentioned in the Life of St Nicholas of Sion; but the identification rests on no more than the similarity of name.

Near the village of Sidek is a rocky eminence with a polygonal wall, an enormous Gothic sarcophagus, and a rock-tomb with Lycian inscription.

Further to the north, above the scattered village of Hacıoğlan, on a hill about 2,000 feet above sea-level on the north side of the stream, is a walled area some 50 yards in length, a fort rather than a city. On the slope towards the stream are three Lycian pillar-tombs; one of them has a diagonal slot in the upper surface, but not large enough for a grave.

The whole of this upland region, even in midsummer, is delightfully cool and green.

CHAPTER TEN

Central Lycia II

APERLAE

A trip by motor-boat along the coast from Kaş to Üçağız and, if desired, on to Demre and Finike, makes a highly enjoyable excursion, and is certainly the most comfortable way of reaching Aperlae. The return trip to Üçağız, with a visit to Simena at Kale, can be done in a long summer day; lodging at Üçağız is somewhat uncertain, as the villagers tend to desert the place in the height of summer. Travellers wishing to stay overnight should make enquiries at Kaş.

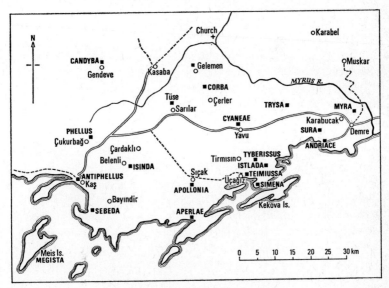

FIG. 12 Map of Central Lycia

There seems no doubt that Aperlae was an old Lycian city. No Lycian inscriptions have been found there, nor are early rock-tombs in evidence; but some fifth-century silver coins inscribed in Lycian APR or PRL must apparently belong to Aperlae. The city is first mentioned in literature by Pliny, then later by the *Stadiasmus*, Ptolemy, and Hierocles. In the Byzantine bishopric lists it appears in the form Aprillae. Post-Lycian coinage is Hellenistic of federal type, and of the third century A.D. under Gordian III. In the time of the Roman Empire Aperlae was at the head of a sympolity including Simena, Apollonia, and Isinda, the four together presumably carrying one vote in the League assembly. How early this arrangement was is uncertain; Apollonia at least seems a very doubtful member in pre-Roman times (see below, p. 104). Citizens of the three associated cities are called officially in the inscriptions 'Aperlite from Simena', etc., and their own ethnics are not used.

The site of Aperlae lies at the head of a long narrow bay, out of the line of sea-traffic, and is today quite uninhabited. As its name, Sıçak Iskelesi, implies, it serves as a landing-stage for the town of Sıçak, something over an hour's walk to the north; but it is very little used. The ruins are on the seaward slope of a low hill just above the north side of the bay.

The original city-wall encloses an area roughly rectangular, extending from the hilltop to within some hundred yards of the water. It is constructed of more or less regular ashlar, topped in places by a late repair in small stones set with mortar. The west wall is the best preserved, standing to a considerable height and containing three gates, two plain and one surmounted by a blind arch (Pl. 52). In the north wall are three square towers. The south wall, running across the slope of the hill, shows also some polygonal masonry; it is now largely destroyed, but about its middle point is a gate which evidently formed the main entrance to the city; it was flanked by a tower on either side. The doorway, over 5 feet wide, is approached by semicircular steps and is surmounted by a massive block 10 feet long, with sockets for hinges on its underside. In the jamb of the door is a large rectangular socket for a bar. Fifty yards to the west of this gate is a comparatively well preserved tower in the

wall; some ten courses of ashlar masonry 3 feet thick are still
standing. The space enclosed by this city-wall is heavily
overgrown and hard to explore; there are numerous remains of
buildings, but nothing identifiable except a small church in the
north-west corner, and in the south-east corner another with
adjacent chapel.

This walled area, then, seems to have formed a sort of
acropolis in ancient times, leaving the harbour area below it
unprotected. At a late date, however, new walls of rubble-and-
mortar masonry were built to run from the east and west ends
of the south wall down to the shore. At the lower end of the
eastern of these walls a new entrance gateway was constructed,
and now stands partly in the water; it was presumably matched
by another on the west, of which nothing now remains.

Outside the early wall, and especially on the east side, are
numerous tombs, nearly all sarcophagi with rounded lid and
crest. Some of them stand between the early wall and the shore,
confirming that this area belongs only to the later fortified city.

But the most interesting discovery at Aperlae in recent times
was made by Robert Carter and his wife. Operating from their
private yacht they observed and later examined very considerable remains of a quay and associated buildings now lying
under water. From the shoreline the bottom slopes very
gradually for about 50 yards to a depth of 6 feet at the actual
quayside, where it drops vertically for another 6 feet. Covering
this shelf is a complex of foundations divided by narrow streets
or lanes; some of the buildings were quite large, but they are
not identifiable. Towards the west end a pier projected out-
wards; to the east of it lies a long stone pierced with a hole at
one end which is likely to have been a mooring-stone. The line
of the quay is stepped in, or indented, at frequent intervals,
generally of about 50 feet, enough no doubt to accommodate a
single ship moored to the quay.

Apart from its position as head of a sympolity, Aperlae was
never a city of much account; in particular, the absence of any
theatre or recognizable temple is significant. The site is very
rarely visited by scholars or tourists, though Carter reports that
in the last year or two parties of local inhabitants have begun
to show some interest.

APOLLONIA

Apollonia, like others of the minor inland towns of Lycia, is not mentioned at all by any ancient writer, unless we may suppose that Stephanus' notice of an island of that name off the coast of Lycia, otherwise unknown, is an error for the city in question. The site is proved by inscriptions on the spot mentioning not only 'Aperlites from Apollonia' but also dedications to Augustus and Tiberius by the People of Apollonia. These last, made independently of Aperlae, suggest that Apollonia was not at that time merely a minor member of the sympolity, but an independent city; similarly, federal coins (very rare) inscribed APO, which can only be of Apollonia, cannot have been struck except by an independent city. Either, then, the sympolity did not exist until the time of the Empire, or Apollonia was not an original member.

The ruins are on a hill some 300 feet high above the village of Sıçak, officially Kılınçlı. They are now easily accessible, as a newly built road passes through Sıçak on its way to Üçağız; it is, however, suitable only for a jeep. The town-walls are well preserved on the west side, and there is a small walled area on the summit, a poorly preserved theatre, a large vaulted reservoir, and numerous cisterns of the familiar bell shape. Tombs are, as usual, abundant, especially on the north slope towards the village, and are mostly of sarcophagus-type. There are, however, six Lycian pillar-tombs, all uninscribed, sufficient by themselves to prove the antiquity of the site, one Lycian rock-tomb with a Greek inscription, and the handsome built tomb shown on Pl. 53. The name Apollonia is of course Greek; what the Lycian name may have been is unknown.

ISINDA

Isinda is no less obscure a city than Apollonia, and is equally unmentioned in antiquity. Like Apollonia also, it is identified by inscriptions naming 'Aperlites from Isinda' found on the site and in the neighbourhood. The ruins are on a hill of moderate height just above the village of Belenli. The ring-wall, quite well preserved in part, is of poor-quality masonry and much repaired. At the highest point is the foundation of a building like a stoa, with steps on the long side and projecting wings at each end. Near the top of the hill are two house-tombs with Lycian inscription. At least two cisterns are to be seen, and on the slope towards the village a number of Gothic sarcophagi with Greek inscriptions.

The inclusion of Isinda at Belenli in the sympolity with Aperlae is surprising, not so much for the distance, which is hardly greater than that between Aperlae and Simena, but because it lies in a quite different region, with the mass of the Kıran Dağ, 2,300 feet high, intervening. An association with Phellus would appear more natural.

Not far from Belenli is the unusual Lycian tomb shown on Pl. 54, half house-tomb, half sarcophagus. The place is known as Çindam, 'the Chinese house', the name apparently applying originally to the tomb.

To the north-east of Isinda a great number of small sites and individual monuments are scattered over the plateau bounded by the Felen-Demre river. No road leads to them, and the writer visited them on foot; whether or not a jeep could reach them he cannot say. A brief account will probably be sufficient.

Close to the village of Çardaklı is a site, apparently a small city-site, but still unidentified. Among its tombs are four with Greek inscriptions either naming the dead man as a Phellite or making the fine payable to Phellus. On the strength of these, Çardaklı was at one time proposed as the site of Phellus.

About half an hour south of Bağlıca is a small fort on a hilltop; the ruins are scattered over the summit, one slope being covered by a mass of fallen blocks. On a little hill close by are some house ruins and a sarcophagus, and about 500 yards to the east is a group of half a dozen sarcophagi, on one of which appears the name Tyinda, presumably the name of the site.

Further north, across the Kaş–Demre main road, near the hamlet of Tüse, is a small town-site on a low hill. The ring-wall is of fairly regular ashlar, enclosing an area some 80 yards long in which are numerous ruined buildings. Below on the south-west side is a Lycian house-tomb built of masonry, with the upper courses stepped pyramid-fashion and a large cap-stone at the top; it is known as Alâdam. There is also a sarcophagus with

Lycian inscription, and half a mile away towards Çerler is a rock-cut house-tomb of normal type but without the usual beam-ends.

A little to the north-east of the village of Gelemen is a well-preserved fort on a low hill. The fort itself is some 50 feet square, divided in two by a cross-wall containing a door and a window; there is another door in the east wall. The masonry is ashlar, bossed and with drafted edges, combed in places. By contrast, the inner face of the west wall is of a curious kind of straggling polygonal of most unusual appearance. The fort is surrounded by a larger walled area, just outside which are a deep cistern and two rock-cut water-tanks. Just to the south are another cistern and some very peculiar rock-cuttings, very hard to understand.

At Gâvuristan, near the village of Uzuncaev, is another small city-site, identified by an inscription as Corba. The wall is partially preserved, in bossed and drafted masonry similar to that at Gelemen. One gate is to be seen, and a Lycian house-tomb, almost entirely buried, with a bilingual inscription.

Close to the tiny hamlet of Avşar, one hour's walk from Sıçak, on the summit of a low hill just to the south, is a tower some 50 by 35 feet, of ashlar masonry heavily bossed and drafted. Adjoining on the west is an area enclosed by a less regular wall, with a well-preserved inner door. Close by are several sarcophagi with Greek inscriptions.

These small sites, remote, not easy to reach, and generally undistinguished, are little known and hardly ever visited; but they show the overall pattern of occupation in this central region. The plateau is dominated by the single city of Cyaneae; all the other cities of any consequence are spread along the coastal strip. Inland there has been for centuries only the one road, and living conditions are not in general very different from what they were two thousand years ago.

CHAPTER ELEVEN

Central Lycia III

THE ROAD NORTH FROM KAŞ, on reaching the top of the ascent from the coast, forks into two; on the right it leads to Cyaneae and Myra, on the left to Kasaba and eventually to Elmalı. This left-hand road is respectable as far as Kasaba, but after that it deteriorates. It crosses a shoulder of the Susuz Dağ at an altitude of close on 5,000 feet. The writer traversed it on a lorry without disaster in 1957, but has had no experience of it since.

CANDYBA

On a mountain-top to the west of Kasaba, reached by a climb of two hours by a good path, is the village of Gendeve, site of the ancient Candyba and preserving the name with little change. Though Pliny includes it among the more celebrated of the Lycian cities, Candyba was never in fact at all distinguished. Its foundation was ascribed to an 'eponymous' hero Candybus, supposed to be the son of Deucalion. Deucalion was the Greek Noah, saved in a boat with his wife Pyrrha from the nine days' flood which destroyed the rest of mankind. Spratt, on his visit to Gendeve in 1842, noticed 'fossils of tertiary origin, which showed that this valley of Kassabar had been, at a recent geological period, an arm of the sea'. It is tempting to imagine some legendary connexion of Candyba with the story of the flood; but there were several heroes called Deucalion in Greek mythology, one of whom was son of Minos, and a connexion with Crete is no doubt more likely (see above, p. 21). A late coin of Candyba shows the figure of a man identified by the inscription as Deucalion, but he carries no attribute which might serve to identify him.

In that part of the inscription on the Xanthian Obelisk which uses the peculiar form of the language (see above, p. 58) there occurs, with variations, a word KÑTABA which seems to be the Lycian name for Candyba. At all events, the antiquity of the city is shown clearly enough by the two rock-tombs with epitaphs in Lycian which have been found on the site. Candyba is mentioned by the geographers, but we learn nothing more of it except that a 'grove of Eunias' in the neighbourhood was much admired. Coins of Candyba are very rare and confined to the time of Gordian III.

The site at Gendeve is now terribly denuded, and its monuments much damaged or destroyed. The acropolis consists of a long narrow summit aligned north–south and something over 200 yards in length; it is enclosed by a dilapidated wall of medieval construction, resting in places upon ancient foundations. Little is to be seen in the interior, though Spratt thought to identify a Christian church. An ancient road, formed by roughly levelling the rock, leads up to the gate on the eastern side. There are several Lycian rock-tombs, now in poor condition, at the base of the acropolis hill, and some sarcophagi. A hollow in the hillside might be the site of a theatre, but if so, it has totally disappeared, as indeed have all the public buildings of the city except for rock-cut foundations at the southern end of the acropolis which have recently been interpreted as a palace and attributed to the fifth or early fourth century.

CYANEAE

Cyaneae is another of the Lycian cities with a Greek name; like Xanthus, that of a colour. The Greek word means 'dark blue', properly the colour of lapis lazuli, though it is freely used by poets to denote any dark colour, for example of the clouds or even the skin of Africans. How or why the city acquired this name is obscure; whether it derives from the Lycian we cannot tell, as the Lycian name is unknown. Cyaneae is also the name of the Symplegades, the Clashing Rocks, at the northern entrance to the Bosporus.

Cyaneae is by its size and by its situation the dominating city of the region. It is listed by all the later geographers, from Pliny onwards, but nothing whatever is said about it, nor do we learn much of its history from the inscriptions. The longest of these is concerned with the honours decreed to a citizen named Jason, son of Nicostratus, a contemporary of Opramoas of Rhodiapolis and, like him, generous with gifts of money to various cities; as many as sixteen of the Lycian cities issued honorific decrees for him at different times. Jason held the title of Lyciarch, and when at the end of his year of office the League assembly voted him the usual honours, objections were raised by a certain Moles, on what grounds we do not learn, and the matter needed to be submitted to the emperor, Antoninus Pius. In his reply the emperor says that he is convinced, by the evidence advanced by the League officials, that Moles' attack was mere calumny, and confirms their grant of honours to Jason.

The site of Cyaneae is abundantly identified by inscriptions. Many of its citizens are named also in numerous other places in all directions, proving its wide influence over the plateau. Though the extant remains are mostly of Roman date, the city's antiquity is sufficiently shown by its Lycian rock-tombs and inscriptions in the Lycian language. It is situated on a steep hill rising some 800 feet from the little plain of Yavu;[1] the climb to the summit takes about 45 minutes, the present path following in part the ancient way up. The top of the hill is surrounded by a wall on three sides enclosing an area some 500 yards in length and breadth; the south side is precipitous and needed no wall. As it stands the wall is late, of poor irregular masonry with many re-used blocks; but the original wall, well built in more or less regular bossed ashlar, is visible in its lower parts on the north and west sides. Three gates, also on the north and west, are still to be seen, and a fourth must be supposed at the south end of the west wall, where an ancient road entered the city. The interior is buried in vegetation and difficult to penetrate; among the many buildings, more or less ruined and lost in the forest, are a library, a baths, a large reservoir arched and plastered, and close by another depot, perhaps for grain rather than water. All over the site are numerous wells and cisterns, mostly bell-shaped.

Just to the west of the acropolis, across a dip in the ground,

[1] Or Yavı, which seems to be the official form of the name; but Yavu is more often heard.

is a lower summit on which stands the theatre. This is of moderate size, with a single diazoma and 25 rows of seats now visible; there were originally a few more. There are five cunei below the diazoma and nine above. On the fifth and ninth rows of the lower block, and on the fifth and tenth of the upper, at intervals of 10 feet or so, holes are cut in the floor and in the seats directly above; these must have held wooden posts, presumably supporting the awning which was spread over the spectators. The retaining wall of the cavea is of small polygonal blocks, presenting a striking appearance, but it has collapsed badly at both ends. Little or nothing is to be seen of the stage-building.

Between the theatre and the acropolis are large numbers of sarcophagi lining a road which entered the city from this side. Sarcophagi are particularly numerous at Cyaneae, especially here and on the way up from Yavu, perhaps more numerous than at any other Lycian city. In the western part they are mostly simple, with rounded lid and crest, but on the eastern slope they are more varied and in some cases adorned with reliefs (Pl. 55). Nearly all are of Roman date.

On the south slope, below the city and on the left of the path up from the village, is a most handsome and interesting group of early tombs. The place is not easy to find without a guide. The tombs are on either side of a passage which may have been part of an ancient road; the rock is levelled in places and cut into steps. On the south side of this, overhanging the steep drop, an outcrop of rock has been carved into the form of a sarcophagus (Pl. 56); the lid, of Gothic-arch shape, has a pair of lions' heads projecting on either side, and figures in relief on the short ends. As the lid is in one piece with the body of the sarcophagus, a rectangular opening is cut in the west end of it to afford access to the tomb. In the lower part of the outcrop are other tombs and rock-cuttings. Behind this group stands a four-sided pillar or stele, visible on Pl. 56; it has an inscription, of which only a few letters can be made out; they are well cut, and might be either Lycian or Greek. In line with it are two rectangular sinkings which appear to have held similar pillars, forming a line of three.

On the other, north, side of the passage are a number of tombs cut in the rock, several bearing Lycian inscriptions. Pl. 57 shows a group at the lower end, picturesque but undistinguished; more remarkable is the tall tomb in Pl. 58. It has the form of a sarcophagus similar to that across the way, but only one short end has been fashioned, projecting as a façade from the rock behind, like the tomb with ox's horns at Pinara (see above, p. 77); and in fact this tomb also had at the apex of the lid a similar emblem, not actually shaped into horns but in the form of an upturned semicircle, one-half of which is now broken away.

In the precipitous south face of the hill, below the city but well up the hillside, is another interesting tomb, conspicuous from the valley but not easy to reach. It has the form of a temple-tomb in the Ionic order; unusually, the porch has a single column between pilasters, with a dentil frieze and pediment above (Pl. 59). The inscription, written in Greek over the door of the main chamber, refers to the upper and lower tombs and to the sarcophagus; the lower tomb is the main chamber itself; by the upper tomb is evidently meant the deep cutting above the pediment, in which a sarcophagus is installed resting on the pediment, a most unusual arrangement. There is also a large rectangular cutting in the rock to the right of the pediment. The sarcophagus was reserved for the owner Perpenenis and his wife, while the rest of the tomb, upper and lower, was for the use of relatives. The inscription further provides that the tomb must not be opened without the consent of the *mindis*; anyone wishing to open it must take the members of the *mindis* along with him, otherwise they may prevent and punish him. Mere permission is not enough; members of the *mindis* must actually be present to see that no impropriety occurs. The present tomb is dated by the style of the script to the third century B.C.[2]

----

[2] For those who are interested, the text concerning the affairs of Jason, son of Nicostratus, is to be found comparatively low down in a gully on the north side of the crest away from the path up from the village. The rock has been cut to form three panels, adorned with *ansae*, which are filled with the writing.

TRYSA

The discovery of Trysa, and in particular of its remarkable heroum, was among the most exciting events in Lycian archaeology. For the present-day traveller the site has lost much of its interest through the removal to Vienna of the principal sculptures, but it has still quite a lot to offer. Trysa is not mentioned anywhere in ancient literature; the name is known only from the inscriptions. Coins of League type inscribed TR may well be of Trysa; the alternative is Trebenna, away in the north-east corner of Lycia.[3]

The site is remote and not easily accessible; it lies on a crest in the eastern part of the plateau near the village of Gölbaşı about 4 miles north-east of Cyaneae. Some of its monuments are among the earliest in Lycia. The ruins extend over an area more than 600 yards in length, partly terraced and enclosed on the north and west by a wall of irregular masonry, patched in places, but not later than the fifth century B.C. On the other sides the wall has disappeared. On the high ground at the west end stood a pillar-tomb, now overthrown and broken, but originally standing some 13 feet high and 4 feet square. The grave-chamber is at the top as usual; below it ran a frieze of warriors and horses, most of which is lost. Standing around are sarcophagi of later date.

The only recognizable public building is a small temple, also near the west end, but it is very badly ruined. From the architectural fragments it appears to have had two columns between antae on the front, though nothing of the columns survives. Numerous pieces were found on the spot of an inscription honouring a citizen who served as priest of Zeus and Helios; the temple may accordingly have been dedicated to one or both of these deities.

Otherwise, apart from a number of cisterns, all the monuments are sepulchral. Most of the sarcophagi are plain, or have bosses in the form of busts or animals' heads; but one in particular is very handsomely decorated (Fig. 13). On one side of the lid are two gorgons' heads with a lion between them, and above this a man in a chariot-and-four between crowns and

[3] Trebenda, a mere dependency of Myra, cannot come in question.

FIG. 13 Trysa. Sarcophagus

masks; he is likely to be the owner of the tomb, the crowns implying that he was a city magistrate. On the other side of the lid are two ox's, or rather cows', heads, and on the short end dolphins and other fishes. There are further reliefs on the crest of the lid: on the left an enormous goose with a man on its back, on the right a galloping rider, and between these a number of men and women; unfortunately the figures are much worn and the scene is hard to interpret.

In another place is a rock-cut stele with the representation of a large dog; apparently the dog protects the grave as he once protected the house.[4] Another relief, which also may be from a

[4] Compare *Turkey's Southern Shore*, pp. 98–9.

H

tomb, shows an ox, a boy, and a man in a long robe raising his
right hand; it has been suggested that the ox is sacrificial and
the man a priest.

But the great glory of Trysa is, or was, undoubtedly the
heroum. This stands at the north-east end of the site and
consists of a sarcophagus, cut from the living rock, in the middle
of an enclosure some 60 feet square. The wall, about 10 feet
high, was covered on its inner face on all four sides of the
enclosure, and on its outer face also on the south side, with a
frieze in two horizontal bands representing scenes from
mythology. Among these are episodes from the *Iliad* and
Odyssey, from the exploits of Theseus, from the Seven against
Thebes, battles of Greeks and Amazons and of Centaurs and
Lapithae, as well as many other figures of doubtful attribution.
These reliefs are now in Vienna. On the terrace below the
heroum are a tall sarcophagus and other tombs. The heroum
itself is dated to the second quarter of the fourth century B.C.

CHAPTER TWELVE

Central Lycia IV

KEKOVA

THE KEKOVA ROADSTEAD is scenically among the most attractive spots on the Turkish coast. It is also the only place in Turkey where the writer has seen flying fish in action. At its head is the village of Üçağız; the name translates the former Greek name of Tristomo, 'the three mouths'. From the inner part of the bay at Üçağız a channel leads to the broader outer part, known as Ölüdeniz, 'the dead sea'; and the whole bay is almost closed by the long narrow island of Kekova Adası. This channel and the two entrances east and west of the island make up the three mouths. The island itself is virtually devoid of antiquities; on the coast overlooking the east entrance is the village of Kale, formerly Kekova, the site of Simena, and at Üçağız are the ruins of Teimiussa. In the bay between the two are a number of islets, some of which have been quarried away almost down to sea-level to provide material for the ancient buildings.

Üçağız, as was mentioned above, may be reached by motorboat from Kaş (or from Demre); but it is now accessible also overland. A forestry road, opened in 1972, leaves the Kaş–Demre road at a point 10 miles from Kaş and leads directly by Sıçak to Üçağız, a distance of 14 miles. This road is at present suitable only for a jeep.

TEIMIUSSA

Teimiussa lies immediately to the east of Üçağız. The name is known only from a single inscription, which designates it as a village; it has accordingly neither a fortification-wall nor any discoverable public buildings. At the edge of the modern village a gate still stands with jambs and lintel intact, and on a low rocky knoll is a tower or small fort hardly larger than a house; otherwise the ruins consist mainly of tombs.

As the visitor proceeds eastward from the landing-stage he will see, a little back from the shore, a pair of rock-cut tombs of house-type, the doors broken wide open; beside that on the right is the standing figure of a young man or boy, and above the door is a Lycian inscription naming the owner as Kluwañimi (Pl. 60). Further to the east across a tiny stream, the ground above the shore is covered with countless sarcophagi jostling one another in picturesque confusion (Pl. 61); some of the larger have an exedra in front. Most of them have Greek inscriptions of Hellenistic or Roman date, in which the persons are named as citizens of Cyaneae or Myra, and the fine for violation is made payable to one of these cities. Teimiussa presumably belonged to one or the other, but it remains uncertain which. Most of the names are Greek, Lycian being in a minority.

At the east end of the site is a delightful little rock-cut quay or landing-stage, unlike anything the writer has seen elsewhere (Pl. 62). It is some 30 yards in length and on average 9 yards wide. The rock-walls are cut vertical and still show the chisel marks; the floor is levelled, but the seaward edge is only roughly shaped. At the east end are cuttings in the floor which at present make shallow pools; their original purpose is obscure. In the back wall is a gate leading through to a kind of sunken road which is little more than a natural cleft; above it on the landward side stands a tomb. The sill of the gate is about 7 feet from the ground, and it is not clear how it was approached; the sill is broken away, but the hinge-holes and bolt-sockets are still to be seen. Also in the back wall is a smaller aperture like a window. There are other tombs above the gate and at the east end of the quay, the latter approached by steps; in both cases the lids are lying overthrown.

SIMENA

Across the bay, a short trip by motor-boat, is the village of Kale, site of Simena, the fourth member of the Aperlite sympolity. The identification is secured by inscriptions found on the spot. The ancient city and modern village are picturesquely mingled and dominated by a finely preserved medieval castle (Pl. 63) whose castellated ramparts rest in part on ancient foundations. The city-wall, of regular ashlar mixed in places with polygonal, stands for long stretches on the southern summit of the hill.

On the sea-shore close to the landing-stage are the ruins of a baths, in polygonal masonry, of modest proportions in fair preservation; it is identified by its dedication to the emperor Titus (A.D. 79–81) by the Council and People of Aperlae and the other members of the sympolity. On the way up from the shore are two large sarcophagi; one is that of Mentor, son of Idagrus, the other has an exedra in front. Higher up, just below the castle wall, stood a stoa attached to a temple; remains of both buildings were noticed in former times, but all that is now to be seen is a few blocks built into a late wall and a fragment of the inscription bearing the name of Callippus.

Inside the castle is a charming little theatre, entirely rock-cut (Pl. 64); it has only seven rows of seats and measures a mere 50 feet in diameter. It cannot have held much over three hundred persons—a fair indication of the very modest size of the city.

On many parts of the site are the ruins of private houses, mostly in polygonal masonry, in some cases converted to modern use. Tombs are not particularly numerous, perhaps two dozen in all; two are rock-cut tombs of house-type, one of which, to the north of the castle, bears a Lycian inscription; the others are sarcophagi, most abundant on the northern summit of the hill.

Simena is certainly among the most attractive of the places in Lycia, both scenically and because the mixture of ancient, medieval, and modern cannot fail to stir a sense of history. But bathers should be wary of sea-urchins.

TYBERISSUS

The little-known and rarely visited town of Tyberissus stands on a hill 1,200 feet above sea-level a few miles to the north-east

of Üçağız and overlooking the plain of Tirmısın (Pl. 65). For
those with motor transport at their disposal the easiest
approach is to drive to Tirmısın and as near to the east end of
the plain as possible; the site is then directly above.

At the foot of the mountain, and little above the level of the
plain, is an attractive glade in which are a dozen or so Lycian
sarcophagi and a number of pigeon-hole tombs. They are dated
by their inscriptions to Hellenistic and Roman times. The fine
for violation is payable to Tyberissus itself or to Myra; Cyaneae,
though much nearer and visible from the hill, does not appear
to be mentioned. Right at the bottom of the glen by the plain
is a more unusual tomb, with two sides, including the door, cut
from the rock, the other two sides having been of masonry.

The main site is on the two summits of the hill. The northern
is the higher and was evidently the acropolis; it carries a fort
of solid, irregular ashlar, with late additions in inferior masonry.
On the saddle between the two summits are the remains of a
building, partly rock-cut, whose doorway, of large squared
blocks, is still standing with the lintel in place.

On the lower southern hill, at its southern end, standing up
to 5 feet in height, is a small church or chapel, little over 20 feet
long, which has replaced a Doric temple. Many blocks of the
temple, some inscribed, have been re-used in it; one, at the
south-east corner, carries part of an honorific decree of the
People of Tyberissus, and another shows that the temple was
that of Apollo, the principal deity of Tyberissus.

Tombs are as usual mostly sarcophagi, but there are two
rock-tombs of house-type, both with inscriptions in Lycian. One
of these is near the top of the hill, at the head of a gully leading
from the south-east; the other is near the foot, close to the plain
of Tirmısın, and carries a relief of two figures, man and woman,
the style suggesting a date not far from 400 B.C.

Pedestrians may descend to Üçağız by a direct path in about
an hour.

Inland from Tirmısın there is a rapid ascent to the high
ground about Yavu. At this higher level, a few miles to the
east, near the village of Hoyran, is an ancient site whose name
still remains unknown. It is unlikely to have ranked as a city,

but the visible remains are interesting and not unimpressive. At
the highest point to the west is the fortified acropolis; on its
east slope are two rock-cut tombs of house-type. One of these
is highly unusual; it is cut from the rock so as to show the front
and one side of the 'house', the side-wall decorated with reliefs.
At the north end of the village is another striking tomb, cut
from an outcrop of rock; it too is of house-type, but above the
row of round beam-ends is a broad frieze adorned with reliefs.
In the middle is a man reclining on a couch; in front of him a
table and four armed men; behind him two male and six female
figures. The pediment above is rounded and carries three more
figures. All the persons but the first are standing. Over the door
is a worn and broken Lycian inscription. Elsewhere on the site
are numerous Gothic sarcophagi and a solid funeral pillar with
a relief of a standing man accompanied by his weapons.

No road leads to Hoyran, and the site would normally be
visited on foot from Yavu.

Even more remote from any road is another small site at the
foot of the great descent from Hoyran, more than a thousand
feet below. The spot is now called Hayıtlı;[1] its ancient name is
revealed by an inscription as Istlada. The ruins lie in a little
valley, hot in summer but most attractive. There are some
remains of a fortification wall, but the principal features are the
houses and tombs. The houses, built of stone, are not apparently
of any very high antiquity, but are unusually well preserved;
in many cases the doorways are still standing, and some at
least had an upper storey. The tombs, many of them perched
on the rocks, are sarcophagi, all of so exactly similar size and
form that they might almost have been cast from the same
mould. One has an inscription—the same that gives the name
of the site—in which the fine of 3,000 drachmae is made payable
'to the People of Istlada for the account of the *xomendys*'. This
curious word, which seems to occur with a similar meaning in
Cilicia, apparently denotes some official body concerned, like
the *mindis*, with the protection of the tomb. The fine is
abnormally high for so small a town. In another case the more
modest fine of 500 denarii is payable to Myra.

[1] From *hayit*, the blue-flowered *agnus castus*.

CHAPTER THIRTEEN

Myra, Sura

MYRA

'Thrice blessed, myrrh-breathing city of the Lycians, where the mighty Nicolaus, servant of God, spouts forth myrrh in accordance with the city's name'. So the emperor Constantine Porphrogenitus describes the city of Myra. And indeed throughout the Middle Ages Myra retained her fame as the see of St Nicholas, now familiar in his transmogrified character of Santa Claus. St Nicholas lived in the fourth century, but before this Myra had been distinguished as a leading city of Lycia, one of the three six-vote members of the League. Rather surprisingly, there is no literary mention of Myra before the first century B.C.; but the surviving monuments and inscriptions leave no doubt of her importance from the fifth century at least. The name Myra was popularly associated with the Greek word for myrrh. Its actual origin is uncertain; it may even be, like Tlos and Patara, a modified form of the Lycian name, which is not certainly recorded. Despite the testimony of Constantine, the city does not in fact seem to have been noted for the manufacture of unguents; indeed, the only product actually recorded is rue.

Myra played little part in history. In 42 B.C., after the capture of Xanthus, Brutus sent his lieutenant Lentulus Spinther to collect money; the Myrans were reluctant and Spinther had to force an entry to the harbour at Andriace by breaking the chain which closed it. The Myrans then submitted and complied with his demands. By the emperors the city was well treated; in A.D. 18 Germanicus, adopted son of Tiberius, with his wife Agrippina, paid it a visit and were honoured with statues erected at Andriace. In A.D. 60 St Paul, on his way to Rome,

changed ships at Myra, that is at Andriace. Dignified by the
title of metropolis, handsomely endowed by gifts of money from
Opramoas of Rhodiapolis and Jason of Cyaneae, Myra was
finally made capital of Lycia by Theodosius II.

The coinage conforms to the normal types in Lycia; federal
issues are reasonably abundant from 168 B.C. onward, and
Imperial issues are virtually confined to the time of Gordian III.
As at Xanthus, it is likely that coins were struck under the
dynasts, perhaps as early as the fifth century.

Myra's neighbour to the east was Limyra, and we learn from
an inscription that there was in Imperial times a ferry service
between the two. This was farmed out annually to private
individuals who were entitled to run it for their own profit; but
it was found that, owing to other persons running unauthorized
pirate services, the bids at the auction were lower than they
should be, and the city treasury was suffering. It was accordingly decreed that anyone making such illegal trips, either from
Myra or from Andriace, should pay to the city a heavy fine for
each journey, and the official contractor should have the right
to confiscate his boat and its tackle. At the same time the
contractor may give permission to others to operate on payment
to him of one-quarter of the fare and of the value of any cargo.
Passage between Myra and Limyra, except for pedestrians, was
naturally effected by sea, as the land route over the intervening
mountain pass is steep, rough, and close on 2,000 feet high.
Fellows calls it 'totally unfit for horses', and Spratt's party, to
save the horses from falling, 'were frequently obliged to push
them from behind or support them by putting our shoulders to
the baggage whilst they were led singly over the steepest and
most difficult places'. Freya Stark rode across successfully,
unencumbered by baggage, and the present writer found no
difficulty on foot. The crossing was certainly used in antiquity,
as there is a fort and a group of sarcophagi at the highest point,
and several towers seem designed to defend it. Today the
traveller drives comfortably round by the new coast road.

The site of Myra lies 1 mile north of the village of Demre
(now officially the *nahiye* of Kale[1]) which preserves the ancient
name; the site itself is known as Kocademre. This region has

[1] To be distinguished from Kale, the site of Simena.

lately become a centre for the growing of tomatoes; from the hills above the whole plain in May and June resembles a vast lake of plastic hothouses (Pl. 68 in the background). To the east the Demre Çayı, the ancient Myrus, reaches the sea down a narrow valley 17 miles long; its wide stony bed serves as a road to the north, but a walk down its length is a harrowing experience not to be recommended. To the west is the harbour of Andriace, 3½ miles from the city by a dead flat road. In 1952 the writer landed at a point on the coast due south of Demre, and reached the village in half an hour's tedious walking over soft sand; but in recent years the old harbour has begun to come again into use.

Strabo describes Myra as standing on a high crest 20 stades from the sea; at present the distance is nearer 30 stades. The high crest must refer to the precipitous hill which rises behind the theatre; some traces of an ancient stepped path lead up it, but on the summit Spratt found nothing but late walls of small stones fitted with mortar. In Strabo's time the inhabited city was certainly on the level ground at its foot. It is now deeply buried and has never been excavated; the visible antiquities consist almost exclusively of the theatre and tombs.

The theatre is large, some 120 yards in diameter, and of Roman type (Pl. 66). The vertical rock-face could not be utilized for the slope of the cavea, which is accordingly wholly built up. The building has recently been cleared and its appearance much improved; the general state of preservation is good. The cavea has a single diazoma with 29 rows of seats below it and six above, with fourteen stairways; it is surrounded by two concentric vaulted galleries, of which the outer was in two storeys. In the west gallery, on the wall between the two corridors or vomitoria, is an inscription reading 'Place of the huckster Gelasius'; we may imagine him at his stall purveying the ancient equivalent of peanuts and iced lollies to the spectators as they flocked in. The diazoma is broad and backed by a 6-foot wall on which are painted names, apparently reserving seats; at the middle point is a projection with steps on either side giving access to the upper seats. On the front of the projection is a figure of Tyche, with the inscription: 'Fortune of the city, be ever victorious, with good luck'. Plate 68 shows the condition of the stage-building after the clearing, with the western parodos and the depth of the Roman stage plainly visible; fragments of the decoration, including broken columns and carved blocks, are lying on the ground. In the orchestra is an interesting inscription concerning imports and exports at Myra, requiring the city to pay to the League treasury 7,000 denarii annually out of the revenues from the import duty.

The famous rock-tombs of Myra are in two main groups. Just to the west of the theatre the steep cliff is honeycombed with closely packed tombs of greatly varying form and size, though the majority are as usual of house-type (Pl. 69). Many of them are quite elaborate, and some are decorated with reliefs in colour. A few are of temple-type, others are extremely simple; sarcophagi are not in evidence. A rather touching graffito on the rock-wall of one tomb records that 'Moschus loves Philiste, daughter of Demetrius'. The tomb shown on Plate 70, and visible also in the corner of Plate 69 at ground-level, is of house-type with a pediment in which are two warriors carrying shields and moving to the left; the man on the right appears to be grasping the other's shield as if to tear it from him. In the middle of the group, about half-way up, are two tombs one above the other, with a third at the side; over the upper tomb is a more elaborate relief showing a man reclining on a couch, with his wife sitting beside him and three armed men, apparently his sons, standing to the left; smaller figures carrying a bowl and (it seems) a double flute approach the bed from the left.[2] The interiors of the tombs also vary greatly in the number and disposition of the benches, some of which are carved to imitate bedsteads.

The second group of tombs is round the corner of the hill facing north-east, and is hardly less impressive than the other (Pl. 71). In order not to lose the sun this group should be visited before 10 o'clock in the morning. Not very much above ground-level, and approached by a somewhat uncomfortable rock-path, is the monument known as the Painted Tomb, certainly one of the most striking in all Lycia. It is of the usual house-type and has in the interior a bench on the right and left sides; in front

[2] This relief is illustrated in Fellows, *Lycia*, p. 200.

is a levelled platform with steps leading up on one side. But the
outstanding feature is the group of eleven life-size figures in
relief. In the porch on the spectator's left is the reclining figure
of a bearded man raising a wine-cup in his right hand (Pl. 73),
evidently the father of the family, and on the opposite wall a
seated woman, presumably his wife, with her children on either
side of her (Pl. 74). On the mullion between the two entrances
to the interior there stood formerly a small paunchy boy facing
left and holding an object resembling a ladle. This figure is said
to have been sawn off by a Greek some hundred years ago and
taken to Athens. On the smoothed rock-face outside the porch
there stands on the left a tall commanding figure, apparently
the same as the reclining figure, but dressed for outdoors with
cloak and a long staff in his right hand (Pl. 72). On the rocks
to the right are five more figures: first a tall female raising her
veil, similarly no doubt identical with the seated woman in the
porch; her daughter stands beside her holding her hand (Pl. 75).
Next, round the angle of the rock, comes a veiled woman,
probably a servant, carrying in both hands a casket towards a
youth who holds out towards her an object, perhaps a flower;
he stands with legs crossed, wearing a cloak and pointed cap,
and leans on a staff propped under his armpit. Behind him is
a smaller figure who seems to be holding the other's cloak in his
right hand (Pl. 76). The identification of this scene is not
entirely clear, but it appears that the figures in the porch
represent the family's indoor life, while those on the rocks
outside show them issuing forth from the house. The three on
the extreme right must then depict a separate scene. At all
events it is clear that there is no question of a family visit to
the tomb; the monument as a whole represents not a tomb but
the family dwelling. The colours, which Fellows saw as red,
blue, yellow, and purple, have now nearly disappeared, apart
from a red and blue background to the reclining man.

   Higher up in the eastern group is a tomb with a pediment
showing a lion savaging a bull; in the porch inside is a scene,
including eight figures, somewhat similar to that on the Painted
Tomb, but on a much smaller scale, and a curious frieze of
fantastic figures, apparently dancers (Fig. 14), on either side of
a lion's head.

FIG. 14 Myra. Decorated Frieze on Tomb

Just to the north of these tombs is the end of an aqueduct
in the form of an open channel cut in the rock about 10 feet
above the level of the plain. The Demre valley begins, at its
north end, near the ruins of a large church which has recently
been excavated; the place is called Dereağzı, the valley mouth.
The stream runs in a delightful gorge between high cliffs among
tall trees, with the path beside it; further south the valley opens
out, the trees and path disappear, and the stream, losing itself
in the shingle, gradually dwindles, at least in summer, to almost
nothing. Fellows and Spratt in March and April found it flowing
generally 4 feet deep in the northern part. How things were in
antiquity is uncertain, but in any case the aqueduct, which is
said to come from a good way inland and was presumably fed
from the river, would serve, rather like a millstream, to bring
the water conveniently to the city, from which the river-bed is
a mile or more distant.

At the west edge of the village of Demre is the famous church
of St Nicholas of Myra, the goal in former times of pilgrims, now
of tourists. Born at Patara about A.D. 300, Nicholas became
bishop of Myra; famous in his own time for the miracles he
performed, he was later the patron saint of Greece and Russia,
as also of children, sailors, merchants, and scholars, and is still
invoked by those unjustly imprisoned, by travellers against the

threat of robbers, and by those in peril on the sea. Sceptics have
indeed questioned his very existence, and it is true that his
achievements, natural and supernatural, are historically un-
authenticated, depending for the most part on Lives of the
saint written long afterwards. We need not doubt that he did
indeed live and die at Myra; for the rest, he who will may
believe what he will. Even his presence at the Council of Nicaea
in A.D. 325, where he is said to have slapped the face of the
heretic Arius so that his bones rattled, is not attested by the
earliest lists.

In the West he is of course best known as Santa Claus, giver
of gifts to children at Christmas time. His patronage of children
derives especially from two of his exploits. It is said that
hearing of a distinguished citizen who had fallen into penury
and was unable to find dowries for his three daughters, Nicholas
secretly by night threw three purses of gold into the house, thus
enabling them to find a suitable marriage; hence the secret
bestowal of presents to children at Christmas. The other story,
that of the Pickled Boys, probably the most popular of the
legends concerning the saint, relates that three lads, wandering
abroad in a time of famine, found their way to the house of a
butcher who murdered them in their sleep, cut up their bodies,
and salted them in a tub, intending to use the flesh in the way
of trade. Nicholas, informed of this occurrence by an angel,
came to the butcher's house and restored the boys to life. This
story, at least in this form, is not in fact told of Nicholas
himself, but seems to be a confusion with a similar miracle
performed by St George.

Many other tales are told of Nicholas's wonderful powers in
rescuing prisoners, shipwrecked sailors, and travellers, parting
the waters of a swollen river, bringing the dead to life, recover-
ing lost property, and in other ways answering the prayers of
the distressed. On occasion he appears as the saviour of his
city; once, again in a time of famine, a fleet of ships carrying
corn from Alexandria to Byzantium called at Andriace;
Nicholas, hurrying to the harbour, ordered the captains to
surrender a hundred bushels from each ship, which they
unwillingly did; when the fleet eventually arrived in the
capital, the cargo was found to be still intact. The corn thus

secured by the saint sufficed the Myrans miraculously for two years and still left enough for sowing.

While still a young man his exceptional nature was equally manifest; when a church in the course of building collapsed and buried him, upon his mother's lamentations the stones fell apart and he emerged unscathed. Even his election as bishop of Myra was not without divine intervention; the dignitaries assembled in the church at Myra to make the choice were instructed by God to elect the man who should first enter the building on the following morning.

When Nicholas died, he was buried in this same church. But the grave did not remain for ever undisturbed. In A.D. 808 the Saracens occupied Myra and their commander is said to have attempted to destroy the tomb, but the saint contrived that he should instead smash another sarcophagus which stood close by. In April 1087, however, a band of men from Bari broke open the tomb and carried off the bones of the saint to Italy. They found the tomb below ground under a pavement which they had to break; after digging down some way they revealed a sarcophagus of brilliant white marble; on smashing its lid they were almost overcome by the powerful fragrance of myrrh, but one of them ventured to plunge his hand in and found the holy bones swimming in the unguent. They were reverently removed and put on board the ship amid the lamentations of the monks. Nicholas himself, however, seems not to have resented these proceedings; while the ship was making halting progress on its way home, he appeared one night to one of the sailors and said: 'Be not alarmed, for I am with you. Be assured that within twenty days we shall be together at Bari'.

By this exploit the men of Bari forestalled the Venetians. These had also been contemplating the theft of the saint's bones; they therefore declined to recognize the removal to Bari, and claimed to have themselves discovered and removed the body at the time of their expedition to Jerusalem during the First Crusade. But no credence is today given to this, any more than to a similar Russian claim. Still less faith, perhaps, will be placed in the scanty assemblage of bones now preserved in a casket in the museum at Antalya and said to have come from the church at Myra. It does seem to be true, however, that the

Venetians did carry off from Myra certain holy relics, including the bones of other persons buried there.

Apart from its sanctity and historical interest, the church as it stands today is not a particularly distinguished building (Pl. 77). Its floor lies 25 feet below the present ground-level, and in the last century was frequently over a foot deep in water. We may well believe that a church has stood on this spot since the third century, but it has undergone many changes in the course of time. An inscription records that it was restored under Constantine IX *anno mundi* 6551, that is in A.D. 1043. In 1034 Myra had again been occupied by the Saracens, who, it may be presumed, were responsible for the destruction. How much of the earlier building remained is uncertain, as there are no clear indications in the present building to distinguish earlier and later masonry. By the mid-nineteenth century the roof had collapsed and the building was half buried, until a further restoration was undertaken with Russian money under an Alsatian director. This work was left unfinished owing to the intervention of the Turkish authorities. Early in the present century the land on which the church stands is said to have been purchased by a Russian consul (other accounts say a Russian princess) with a view to reanimating the cult of the saint, but this too was thwarted by the Porte. The present upper storey and bell-tower are quite modern.

The church is in basilica form, with three aisles, to which a fourth has at some time been added on one side. In the apse at the end of the central aisle or nave is a synthronon with a covered passage running round and a stone placed as an altar. On the west are a narthex and exonarthex, and pleasant cloisters on the north side. The walls contain re-used material including fragments of inscriptions.

The monument displayed and venerated for many centuries as the tomb of St Nicholas himself is shown in Fig. 15. It consists of a plain marble sarcophagus in a niche, fenced off by a decorated marble screen between pillars. The men of Bari found their tomb underground beneath a stone pavement; if this account is true, either the sarcophagus has been removed from its original place or this is not the tomb which they opened. Others besides Nicholas were buried in the church. At

60 Teimiussa. Lycian tomb.

61 [*overleaf*] Teimiussa. Necropolis.

62 [*overleaf*] Teimiussa. Quay.

61

62

63

64

65 Tyberissus and the Plain of Tırmısın.

63 [*overleaf*] Simena. The Castle.

64 [*overleaf*] Simena. Theatre.

66 Myra. Theatre.

67 Myra. Sculptured masks.

68 Myra. Theatre.

69 Myra. Western group of tombs.

71 Myra. Eastern group of tombs.

70 Myra. Tomb in the western group.

73 Myra. 'Painted Tomb'.

72 Myra. 'Painted Tomb'.

75 Myra. 'Painted Tomb'.

74 Myra. 'Painted Tomb'.

77 Myra. Church of St. Nicholas.

76 Myra. 'Painted Tomb'.

78 Myra. Mausoleum at Karabucak.

79 [*opposite*] Arycanda. Stadium.

80 [*opposite*] Arycanda. Newly excavated temple.

83 Limyra. Late Lycian tomb.

81 [*opposite*] Limyra. Tombs in the hillside.

82 [*opposite*] Limyra. Late Lycian tombs.

84 Limyra. Lycian sarcophagus.

85 Limyra. Newly excavated mausoleum.

FIG. 15 Myra. The Reputed Tomb of St Nicholas

the same time it is recorded that a certain Mitylenean presbyter in the ninth century set out for Myra with the intention of doing reverence 'to the precious coffin' of St Nicholas and collecting from it myrrh for the protection of his family; this certainly suggests a tomb accessible above ground. On the other hand, the tomb which is shown to visitors nowadays as that of the saint is far from authentic. It is an ornate sarcophagus, badly broken and clumsily patched, with a lid on which repose a husband and wife. Such a lid is obviously inappropriate, though it might have been taken from elsewhere and added simply for completeness. The matter therefore remains in some uncertainty.

The port of Andriace nowadays presents in summer quite a lively scene, being popular for picnics and for bathing, to which the Turks have taken more and more in recent years. Just to the north a stream of remarkably cold water enters the sea. The road from Myra is lined with numerous sarcophagi, many of them now almost buried in the sandy ground. Ruins of several large Roman buildings stand on the hillside to the north, and

I

a tower on the headland to the south of the harbour. But the most notable building is the granary of Hadrian, some distance from the sea on the south side. It is very similar, both in size and in form, to that at Patara (see above, p. 89), having eight rooms entered by separate doors from the north front, and communicating by smaller doors set near the front wall. The pediment, which ran the whole length of the building, is preserved only at the west end, where part of the Latin dedication survives. Busts of Hadrian and the elder Faustina stand over the central entrance, and several carved blocks are built into the front wall; one of these, to the left of the second door from the west, shows Serapis standing and Pluto reclining, with a griffin between them; the inscription relates that it was dedicated in obedience to a dream by an officer of the granary. In the same wall is an inscription of early Byzantine date recording the construction, in accordance with standards sent from Byzantium, of weights and measures for the cities of Myra and Arneae. A little in front of the granary is a wall of good squared blocks which originally carried statues of the emperors.

SURA

Sura lies to the west of Myra, an hour and a half on foot, but only quite a short walk from the nearest point of the road. The site is just beyond the *mahalle* of the same name. Sura was never an independent city, but merely a dependency of Myra; it is hardly mentioned except in connexion with its fish-oracle, which, however, had considerable notoriety and is described in some detail in the ancient literature. At the extreme end of a plain some half a mile in length is the tiny 'acropolis', rising little more than 30 feet above the level of the plain; a dozen or so Gothic sarcophagi are scattered around. On the hill is a rock-cut house-tomb with Lycian inscription, and at the south-west corner is a conspicuous statue-base with a very long Lycian inscription of which only a few letters of each line remain. On the south side is a row of rock-cut stelae with lists of clergy attached to the cult of Apollo Surius.

But the chief interest of the site lies in the temple and oracle of Apollo. Immediately to the west of the acropolis the ground falls steeply for several hundred feet to the head of a marshy inlet. The temple stands close to the edge of the marsh; it is quite small and in fair preservation. Carved on its interior walls are a number of inscriptions recording devotions paid by suppliants; oddly enough, they are not offered to Apollo Surius but to the Anatolian horseman-god Sozon, and in one case to the Rhodian deity Zeus Atabyrius. Close by are the extensive ruins of a Byzantine church which has, as so often, succeeded to the pagan temple and prolonged the sanctity of the place into medieval times.

Concerning the fish-oracle itself we have quite detailed information. Pliny says:

> At Myra in Lycia at the fountain of Apollo whom they call Surius, the fish, summoned three times on the pipe, come to give their augury. If they tear the pieces of meat thrown to them, this is good for the client, if they wave it away with their tails, it is bad.

Plutarch says that the diviners sit to watch the fish as they would birds of omen, and decide the augury according to fixed rules or by commonsense, observing how the fish twist and turn, pursuing or fleeing from one another. But the fullest account comes from Polycharmus. He speaks of a well of sea-water at a place called Surius, and says:

> When they come to the sea, where is the grove of Apollo by the shore, on which is the whirlpool on the sand, the clients present themselves holding two wooden spits, on each of which are ten pieces of roast meat. The priest takes his seat in silence by the grove, while the client throws the spits into the whirlpool and watches what happens. After the spits are thrown in, the pool fills with sea-water, and a multitude of fish appear as if by magic, and of a size to cause alarm. The prophet announces the species of the fish and the client accordingly receives his answer from the priest. Among smaller fish there appear sometimes whales and sawfish and many strange and unknown kinds.

This is confirmed by Artemidorus, who records that

the local people say that a spring of sweet water wells up, and
this causes whirlpools in which large fish appear; to these the
clients throw their offerings of boiled or roast meat, cakes or
bread. The harbour and the place of the oracle are called
Whirlpool.

These accounts are at variance in one respect only, namely
whether it was the species of the fish or their behaviour which
determined the favourability of the oracle. We may also
distrust the whales and sawfish, though of course sharks are not
unknown on the Turkish coasts. But in all other respects it is
interesting, indeed fascinating, to observe how exactly the
present conditions illustrate the ancient accounts. The 'harbour'
is the marshy inlet, which was undoubtedly sea in antiquity;
the fountain of Apollo is still there, a fine abundant spring which
issues from the foot of the hill a few paces from the temple and
quickly forms a good stream which flows through the marsh to
the present sea-coast a mile or so distant. Just in front of the
temple a number of springs well up in the stream—that is, in
the sea in antiquity—giving a swirling effect to the surface of
the water; this agrees exactly with the local inhabitants'
account of the 'whirlpool', and explains the curious expression
'a well of sea-water'. Even the mysterious filling of the pool
could be managed easily enough by the priest by means of some
apparatus to control the fountain of Apollo. There are not now,
so far as the present writer could see, any actual structural
remains that could be associated with the oracle, but they would
hardly be expected to survive.

Visitors to the oracle should be warned against attempting
the walk along the edge of the marsh to Andriace and Myra, as
the writer did in 1960; the 'path' of which the guide spoke
proved to be a matter of scrambling or jumping from rock to
rock. A mile of this is more than most people would claim to
enjoy.

Between Myra and Sura, close beside the present road at
Karabucak, is the notable monument shown on Plate 78. It is
a mausoleum of Roman date, built entirely of masonry and in
quite good preservation, standing in part to its full height of

some 40 feet. The door on the north is high and handsomely
decorated with mouldings; it is flanked on the left by a
Corinthian pilaster to which another, now lost, corresponded on
the right. The east and south interior walls have large false
arches; the west side is largely destroyed. Otherwise only the
roof is lacking. The tradition of the Lycian rock-tombs is
preserved in the benches round the walls inside, and in the two
vaulted hyposoria entered from the back.

K

CHAPTER FOURTEEN

Arneae, Arycanda

ARNEAE

From Demre a newly constructed road leads up to the high
ground beyond the Demre Çayı to the north as far as Muskar.
Scattered ruins around this and the neighbouring village of
Gödeme include sarcophagi whose inscriptions show that this
was Myran territory. Three hours to the north of Muskar is the
village of Çağman, with a coffee-house attractively placed under
huge plane-trees, and a badly damaged Lycian house-tomb.
Half an hour to the west of the village is a hill known as
Güceymen Tepesi, on which are abundant sherds, part of a
ring-wall, and a fragment of an honorary decree issued by 'the
People', and low down on the slope of the adjoining hill is
another house-tomb with a long Lycian inscription over the
entrance. Here is clearly the site of a small town, though surely
not entitled to the rank of a city; the epitaph of an Arneate in
the village of Çağman indicates that we are here on the
territory of Arneae.

On the way from Muskar to Çağman, near the hamlet of
Karabel, are the considerable ruins of a Christian church, and
some 4 miles to the east, far from any road, in a valley on the
south slope of the Alaca Dağ, is a still better-preserved church
with adjoining buildings; an inscription records its restoration
anno mundi 6320 (or A.D. 812), four years after the Saracen
assault on the tomb of St Nicholas at Myra. A mile or so away
is a group of ancient houses and several Lycian sarcophagi.

Arneae is among the most isolated of the Lycian cities, and
even today is not easily accessible. A road branches westward
from a point about 2½ miles south of Aykırca and leads by Yazır
to Kaş Kasaba, passing close to Ernes; it is of poor quality, but
quite how poor the writer cannot say, having never traversed

it. Arneae lies just to the south of Ernes; the survival of the name is evident. The city is barely mentioned in the ancient literature and has no history whatever. As so often, all that we know of it is derived from the inscriptions and the ruins themselves. All travellers who have visited it have been impressed by the beauty of the scenery and the varied vegetation. The antiquity of the city is assured by an inscription in the Lycian language, and other inscriptions show that it stood at the head of a sympolity of towns, whose citizens are designated in the normal manner as 'Arneate from such-and-such a place'. One of these associated towns is named as Coroae; another is surely represented by the site at Çağman— if this is not Coroae itself, which there is no reason to suppose. The association with Myra continued into Byzantine times, when Arneae was the see of a bishop ranking ninth under the metropolitan of Myra. Coinage is confined to the time of Gordian III.

The site is strongly protected by nature. On three sides the hill falls steeply away, and on the north a jumble of rocks and boulders makes the approach from the village difficult and painful. On the way up are two Lycian rock-tombs, one on the left of the path and the other, with Lycian epitaph, on the right. The top of the hill is enclosed by a ring-wall surviving in large part, but much repaired in later times; it has half a dozen towers and at least two gates. In the interior are two churches in reasonable preservation, and traces of houses and other buildings. Very little remains from earlier times; in addition to the Lycian rock-tombs, one or two sarcophagi, and some parts of the ring-wall, there are a score of inscriptions of Roman date mostly built into the wall. One of these records the conversion to a public guest-house of a former gymnasium, and its dedication to the emperor Trajan, but this is not identifiable on the site. Another is an *ex-voto* dedication to a local deity by the name of Tobaloas.

ARYCANDA

Unlike Arneae, Arycanda may be reached without any trouble at all. The site lies an easy fifteen minutes' walk from Aykırca,[1]

1 Or Aykırıçay, or Aykırçay.

a stopping-place on the main road from Elmalı to Finike. Aykırca is an attractive spot, with a fine cascade of ice-cold water falling from high rocks, and a couple of Lycian rock-tombs close above the road, though its beauty is somewhat spoiled by the lorries and other vehicles which are generally assembled at the coffee-house. The river, the ancient Arycandus, runs in a deep gorge below. The scenery made a great impression on Fellows: 'All', he says, 'is grand, yet lovely'.

The character of the Arycandans did not, it seems, match the beauty of their surroundings. Their prodigality, we learn, their profligacy, sloth, and love of pleasure led them into debts which they could not pay; so, when Antiochus III was engaged in taking Lycia from the Ptolemies in 197 B.C., they associated themselves with his cause, hoping to be rewarded by the remission of their obligations.

We are further informed that Arycanda possessed a sanctuary of Helios at a spot called first 'the Prow', later 'the Warship', on account of the formation of the ground. This is one of the few relics of Rhodian rule in Lycia, for Helios was above all a Rhodian deity. The place itself has not been identified.

For the rest it appears that Christianity had a hold in the city by the end of the third century, for a copy was found there of a petition to the emperor Maximinus, a persecutor of the Christians, from the province of Lycia and Pamphylia, requesting that these 'illegal and abominable practices of the godless' be denounced and suppressed. Later Arycanda was the seat of a bishopric.

Although the antiquity of the city is sufficiently proved by the termination of the name in -anda, by the Lycian rock-tombs mentioned above, and by the inclusion of the word 'Lycian' on its federal coins, no inscriptions in the native language have been found on the site. In this the case of Arycanda resembles that of Patara.

The site itself is an unusual one, being set on a steep hillside, reminiscent of Delphi in many respects. Overhung by rocky heights, it is militarily indefensible and seems indeed never to have been protected by a wall; the Arycandans were evidently as unwarlike as they were unthrifty. The acropolis, if such it can be called, is at the very foot of the site, just on the right of the path from Aykırca; it is no more than a knoll and carries only a ruined tower.

But the other ruins are quite considerable. Across the stream-bed the eye is caught by the baths, an imposing building with a front a good 30 feet high, two rows of three windows, and an apse at one end with another window. But the different rooms are hardly identifiable in their present condition.

The theatre is on the small side, in the Greek style with little or no sign of Romanization. The cavea has collapsed in the middle, but the two wings are standing and some of the seats; the retaining wall is of mixed ashlar and polygonal masonry, the

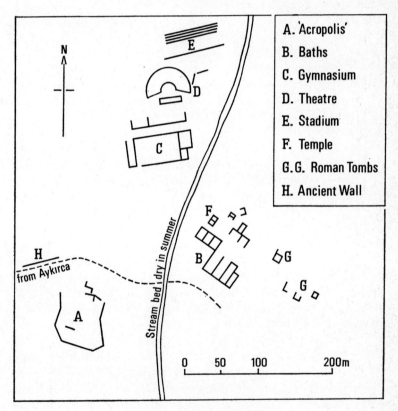

A. 'Acropolis'

B. Baths

C. Gymnasium

D. Theatre

E. Stadium

F. Temple

G.G. Roman Tombs

H. Ancient Wall

FIG. 16 Plan of Arycanda

analemma of smooth-faced ashlar. The stage-building is in fair
preservation; the outline of a long rectangular building is
discernible, with one door in the back wall and one in the front
wall (leading on to the stage) still standing complete with lintel.
The front of the stage itself is visible at the east end, hardly
6 feet from the stage-building; even for a Hellenistic stage this
is remarkably narrow. The parodoi remain open in the Greek
manner. The theatre has recently been excavated by an
expedition from Ankara University.

Below the theatre is a good-sized building with a massive wall
of large polygonal blocks, with three arches; it has been called
a gymnasium, but it has not been excavated and the identification is not certain.

Behind the theatre is a high terrace-wall of very mixed
masonry above which is the stadium, recently cleared and very
attractive (Pl. 79). There are seats only on the north side; four
or five rows are preserved, and there can never have been many
more. The arena is about 18 yards wide, and at present only
80 or 90 yards long, or less than half the length of a normal
full-sized stadium; but the original length is uncertain, as the
west end is buried under earth and stones which have slipped
down the hill.

A short way above the baths is a small temple (F) which has
recently been excavated by a Turkish party from Ankara. It is
a simple but handsome building of carefully cut marble blocks,
in the Corinthian order, comprising a pronaos and a cella. The
pronaos, on the west, is standing in large part; it has two antae,
one of which is preserved complete with its capital (Pl. 80).
There are no steps in front, nor any evident means of entering.
From the pronaos a high moulded door leads to the cella; its
richly decorated lintel-block lies beside it. A few drums of
Corinthian columns are lying around, but the cella walls are now
little above ground. The temple has at a later time been used
for other purposes; the cella has been divided up by two
longitudinal walls, into one of which (on the right) has been
built a fragmentary epitaph in rough script. By the left-hand
wall is lying a broken sarcophagus, and on the south wall of the
pronaos is a cross with the familiar inscription 'Jesus Christ is
victorious'. It seems not unlikely that the building was used in

Byzantine times as a place for Christian worship; no church has been identified elsewhere on the site.

To the south-east of this, close above the baths, are a number of built tombs of Roman date; it has indeed been suggested that the building just described was in fact not a temple at all, but a tomb. The largest and finest of these tombs, on the plan, has an elegantly decorated door, with a relief above showing a bull's head with a winged figure on either side; in the interior the roof is arched, and there are benches on three sides. By the path leading east from the city are other built tombs which evidently lined a street approaching from that side. Once handsome, they are now in ruins.

To the east of Arycanda is a group of three cities, modest, little known, remote from any road, and requiring considerable effort to reach. They are Idebessus, Acalissus, and Cormi. In the Roman Imperial age they were united in a sympolity, with Acalissus at the head. The first two names, with their termination in -ssus, go back to the time before the Greeks came to Lycia; but despite their antiquity no Lycian rock-cut tombs or inscriptions are found in either of the cities. The sympolity was included in the Lycian League, and its citizens held federal offices in the second and third centuries A.D.; Acalissus, as the head of the union, struck coins under Gordian III and was the recipient of a gift of money from Opramoas.

Of the three Idebessus is the most rewarding to the enterprising traveller who makes his way there. It lies very high, close on 3,000 feet above the sea, at Kozağacı, a *mahalle* of Karacaören. The writer went up to it in 1953 from Arycanda, and this was the most exhausting day's walk that he remembers in his time in Turkey. The track is rarely used, virtually non-existent in places, and a guide was hard to find; eventually an old man who had followed it twenty years before and thought he could find it, volunteered to serve. The journey, barely a dozen miles as the crow flies, took nearly all day. Freya Stark did it in the reverse direction, and even downhill found it hard going.

Idebessus stands on a narrow ridge running north–south parallel to the mountain-face of Bey Dağ. There are remains of a fortification wall along the ridge and on the outer, east, slope of it, but most of the buildings are on the inner slope. The theatre, facing west towards the mountain, is tiny, barely a hundred feet in total diameter, and might hold some 600 or 700 people. The cavea, with two stairways, is badly ruined, and there seems never to have been a permanent stage-building. Some hundred yards to the north of the theatre are the rather undistinguished ruins of a baths, fed by an aqueduct of which the substructure is visible approaching from the north. To the north again is a medieval basilica, but this too is in poor condition.

The most attractive feature of Idebessus is certainly its tombs, which are numerous and very fine. They are not grouped in a necropolis but scattered all among the city buildings from end to end of the site, one group being within a few yards of the theatre. They are all, or almost all, of sarcophagus-type with the rounded and crested lid which is characteristic of the later period, but the lids are in many cases removed. The commonest decoration is a round shield, but some tombs have handsome reliefs, including garlands carried by cupids, cupids playing with dogs, hares, and other animals, wild beasts fighting among themselves, and a lion savaging a humped bull. In some cases the sarcophagi stand on solid bases with an exedra in front. Spratt speaks of a single uninscribed rock-tomb, which the writer has not seen.

Acalissus lies lower down to the east of Idebessus, at an uninhabited spot called variously Gâvuristanlık or Asarderesi. The ruins are meagre in the extreme. Apart from an assortment of walls of varying antiquity and the relics of two churches, they consist of some thirty sarcophagi whose inscriptions give the name of the city, and a few plain rock-tombs in the hill to the north. There is also the base of a statue of the emperor Commodus (A.D. 180–192), with an inscription in which the title *neocorus* has been added subsequently to the city's name.

Cormi is situated on the other side of the Alâkır river, close to its eastern bank and not far from the village of Karabük. The writer in 1953 came down to the river from Acalissus, but found it flowing deep and strong and was unable to make the crossing on foot. From the scanty descriptions available it appears that the city is small, the ruins consisting of a ring-wall round the hill, and in the interior some half-dozen inscribed statue-bases and other stones. The usual sarcophagi seem to be lacking.

Two of the inscriptions give the name of the city (which is otherwise utterly unknown), but only in the form of the ethnic. The termination of the name is accordingly uncertain, nor is it sure whether it is Greek or native. *Kormos* is the Greek for a lopped tree-trunk, and it may be that the city is a Greek foundation, named from the original settlers' log-houses, of the kind imitated in the Lycian house-tombs. But it is equally possible that the name was Corma and not Greek at all.

Among the inscriptions are a fragmentary decree of the Roman Senate dating to 80 B.C., apparently referring to the settlement of Lycia after the first Mithridatic War, and an honorific decree of the People of Cormi for a citizen who seems to have saved the city from war and danger and preserved the democracy. The war in question appears to be that against the pirate chief Zenicetes in 78 B.C.,[2] so that these two texts are the only documents found in the three cities of the sympolity which are earlier than the Christian era.

[2] See *Turkey's Southern Shore*, pp. 33, 156.

CHAPTER FIFTEEN

Eastern Lycia

LIMYRA

East of Finike the mountains recede somewhat from the shore, leaving an extensive coastal plain, whose oranges, until the advent of the 'Washington', were reckoned the finest on the Istanbul market. This plain is watered by two considerable rivers: at the west end the Arycandus, known in this part as the Yaşgöz Çayı, and further east the Alâkır Çay. The latter has often been identified with the ancient Limyrus, but this is open to question. Strabo says that if you go up on foot for 20 stades (rather over 2 miles) from the mouth of the Limyrus, you come to the town of Limyra. Pliny speaks of 'Limyra, with a river into which the Arycandus flows'. These accounts do not at all fit the Alâkır Çay, but they do very well describe a third stream, the Göksu, which rises from an abundant spring among the ruins of Limyra and joins the Yaşgöz Çayı close to Finike; the distance from Limyra to the sea is now about $3\frac{1}{2}$ miles, or considerably more than 20 stades. If Pliny's river is the Limyrus, as would naturally be supposed, the case is conclusive; but he does not actually name it. Strabo's words would normally imply that Limyra was on the river 20 stades from the mouth; but why does he add 'on foot'? Does he mean simply that the river is not navigable? Or is he thinking of the distance across country direct from the river-mouth to the city? It is uncertain where the river-mouth lay in his day, as the coast has surely silted up in the meantime, so that 20 stades might be more or less correct. It is not impossible therefore that the Alâkır is the Limyrus and the Göksu nameless. The present writer confesses to a preference for the other view; the name Limyrus seems particularly suitable for a river which, short though it be, rises actually in Limyra. But it must be admitted that in this case the much greater Alâkır, over 40 miles long, remains without an ancient name.[1]

A little, but not much, is said about Limyra in antiquity. It is named as one of the towns which surrendered to Antiochus in 197 B.C., and in A.D. 4 Gaius Caesar, grandson and adopted son of Augustus, died there on his way back to Rome from Armenia, where he had been treacherously wounded at a conference. In earlier times, however, Limyra had enjoyed a period of importance, for it seems to have been, in the fourth century, the capital city of the dynast Pericles, whose energetic and ambitious activities were mentioned above (p. 25). A number of inscriptions at Limyra (and elsewhere) contain the phrase *periclehe kñtawata*, which is interpreted to mean 'general of Pericles'. It is virtually certain that the splendid heroum recently discovered at Limyra was in fact his tomb (see below, p. 145).

Pliny says that there was at Limyra an oracular fountain whose responses were given by fish; if they seized the food thrown to them, it was a good omen, if they waved it away with their tails, it was bad. The remarkable identity of this mode of divination with that practised at Sura has led many scholars to suppose that Pliny, or his source, has given us the same information twice, confusing L*imyra* with *Myra*. It is noticeable, however, that he adds the observation that the fountain moves about from place to place, taking the fish with it; with the abundance of springs at Limyra this is perhaps not impossible, but at Sura it is out of the question. Moreover, oracles were almost certainly given at Limyra, since the word 'oracle' appears on its Imperial coins. Perhaps then we may accept Pliny's statement as it stands.

From inscriptions recently found on the site we learn that the principal deity at Limyra was Olympian Zeus. Athletic festivals were celebrated in his honour, and his thunderbolt is a frequent type on the coins. Elsewhere in Lycia Zeus is by no means prominent as compared with his offspring Apollo and Artemis.

---

[1] The *Stadiasmus* reckons 60 stades from Gagae to the mouth of the Limyrus, that is to a point just about half-way between the Alâkır and the Göksu. This is hardly helpful.

144 LYCIAN TURKEY

A visit to Limyra poses no problems. The road from Finike to Kumluca passes through the middle of the site.[2] The inhabited city lay at the foot of the long south slope of the Tocak Dağ, with a fortified acropolis on the crest above. The hillside rises at an angle of 30 degrees, and is split vertically into an endless series of striated ridges; in the faces of these ridges, generally the east face, are cut countless tombs (Pl. 81). At the foot of the hill, close beside the road, is the theatre, small but in very fair condition, with a disproportionately large orchestra. The cavea has a single diazoma, with sixteen rows of seats below it and rather more above; its retaining wall is of handsome bossed masonry. The diazoma is backed by a wall 5 feet high, behind which a covered passage runs all round the cavea, with openings to the diazoma. On either side of the orchestra is a large vaulted entrance, but of the stage-building only some shapeless lumps and a few carved blocks remain. The date of the building is known quite closely;[3] about A.D. 140 Limyra received from Opramoas a sum of at least 20,000 denarii expressly for the construction of a theatre.

Apart from the theatre little remains of the city itself. The acropolis carries some relics of a ring-wall with recognizable gates, but nothing survives in the interior beyond a few rock-cuttings. Trial trenches, however, have shown that there was perhaps a settlement here in the fourth century B.C. On the plain are the ruins of several massive buildings, unidentified and of dubious antiquity, and an old Turkish convent pleasantly situated beside the stream which is probably the Limyrus.

The main feature of Limyra is the tombs, several hundred in number and collected in six main groups continuing far to the east of the city. They are thickest near the foot of the hill, but extend quite a long way up. To visit even a quarter of them is a difficult and time-consuming business, as they are not all easy to find and the ridges are tiresome to cross. It is best, if possible, to find a guide who knows the position of some of the more handsome specimens, unless the visitor is prepared to spend several days on the site. Most of the tombs are of Lycian

[2] In 1972 this road was blocked at a point beyond Limyra, and Kumluca was reached by another road along the beach.
[3] As at Tlos, above, p. 67.

house-type (Pl. 82), but they vary greatly in form and in decoration. Some are quite plain, others are adorned with handsome reliefs of similar style to those at Myra, and there are several fine sarcophagi (Pl. 84). In the western part of the city stood a tower-like tomb, now below the water-table, dated by its rich ornamentation to the time of Augustus. There seems no doubt that this is, or was, a cenotaph erected to the memory of Gaius Caesar; the numerous fragments found by the excavators suggest that the decoration represented his exploits.

But no doubt the most interesting of all the tombs is the heroum or mausoleum recently discovered high up the hillside at its west end. A path leads up to it from the village below; the ascent direct from the theatre across the ridges is tougher than it looks and is definitely not recommended. The monument is completely destroyed down to its lowest parts (Pl. 85), but many of its architectural features were found in the excavation and are collected in the depot (locked) on the spot. It stands on a terrace some 60 feet square constructed for it; on this is a solid rock-base about 18 inches high, round the edges of which a number of moulded orthostates remain in position. The tomb was in two parts, a lower grave-chamber (though without an occupant) and an upper chamber in the form of a temple in the style called 'amphiprostyle', that is with a row of columns at front and back only. Here, however, the columns were replaced by caryatids, four in each row. Two of these may be seen through the grille of the depot; they are impressively tall. There too are several blocks of the frieze which adorned the cella; it showed the hero mounting his chariot and followed by his armed forces, some on foot, some on horseback. Both Greek and Persian influence is detectable in the figures. The central acroterium of the pediment represented Perseus and the Gorgon, and in this also a Graeco-Persian element is discernible; the Persians claimed to be descended from the Argive hero Perseus, and the Argives in the early fifth century made a treaty of friendship with Xerxes. The style of the monument as a whole dates it to the early fourth century, and illustrates the position held by Lycia at that time, intermediate between East and West.

RHODIAPOLIS

East of Limyra the Lycian character of the ancient cities
becomes noticeably less conspicuous. Their foundation-legends
are Greek, and in particular Rhodian. Rhodiapolis actually
means 'Rhodian city'; Corydalla was called by Hecataeus,
about 500 B.C., 'city of the Rhodians'; Gagae is said to have
been, and Phaselis surely was, founded by Rhodians. Olympus
seems to have been a later foundation. It is true that most of
these legends may be, and have been, called in question; the
story of Gagae is fairly obviously mythical; Hecataeus may
have meant by 'Rhodians' merely the people of the neighbouring Rhodiapolis; and Rhodiapolis itself is said by Theopompus
to have been called after Rhode, daughter of Mopsus. However
this may be, it is certain that east of the Alâkır Çay the
characteristic types of Lycian tomb, apart from some late
sarcophagi at Rhodiapolis, are not to be seen, and only three
inscriptions in the Lycian language, two at Rhodiapolis and one
from Corydalla, have hitherto been discovered. All the cities,
however, were included in the Lycian League, and the federal
coins of Rhodiapolis and Gagae at least bear the title 'Lycian'
which is accepted as denoting that the city was regarded as
truly Lycian by race.

The natural centre for visiting these cities is Kumluca. A
visit to Corydalla is indeed easy, as the site lies a comfortable
fifteen minutes' walk to the west, but it is scarcely rewarding
as the city no longer exists. Spratt in 1842 saw quite considerable ruins, including a theatre and aqueduct and remains of
many buildings of varying antiquity covering two low conical
hills; of all this nothing whatever survives except the hollow of
the theatre on the southern hill and a few scattered stones.
When the writer was there in 1952, he found a constant stream
of lorries carrying away stones (quite illegally, but a blind eye
was evidently being turned), and Kumluca itself, and the
neighbouring villages of Haciveliler, Çalka, and Hızırkâhya,
were full of the dismembered remnants of Corydalla. Many of
these blocks were inscribed, and one, built into a new house in
Kumluca, carried a bilingual in Lycian and Greek.

Rhodiapolis may be reached direct from Corydalla in about

an hour's rather toilsome climb on foot, but if a jeep is available, a more comfortable approach can be made by driving out from Kumluca on the Gödene road for about a mile, then turning left on the Sarıcasu road for something over 2 miles, after which there is a pleasant walk up in 45 minutes by a good and easy path. A guide is of course necessary. The site is on a hilltop shaded and scented by pines, and is quite delightful.

The feature which at once attracts the visitor's attention is the great number of buildings, still standing, constructed of small stones with or without cement. They are of varying sizes, some evidently private houses, others of uncertain destination; they are likely to be of late Roman date (Pl. 86). In the centre of the city is the theatre; this is small, some 130 feet in width, and faces south; sixteen rows of seats are preserved, without a diazoma (Pl. 87). Part of the stage-building remains; the line of blocks marking the back of the stage is still in place, with a door leading under it to the stage; the stage itself is not preserved. The cavea is rather more than a semicircle, and the parodoi seem always to have remained open; there is in fact little evidence of Romanization.

Close behind the stage-building is the famous monument of Opramoas, famous because its walls were covered with inscriptions recording honours of various kinds paid to him, the whole comprising the longest inscription in Lycia, and probably in the whole of Asia Minor. Opramoas was a millionaire, a citizen of Rhodiapolis, in the time of Antoninus Pius (A.D. 138–161); he held high office in the Lycian League and was exceptionally generous in his gifts of money to almost all the cities of Lycia. The monument is his tomb, some 25 by 22 feet, of well-squared blocks, with a handsomely decorated doorway, but it is now in complete ruin and the blocks scattered; only a few pieces of the walls can still be seen. The inscribed documents consist of letters from the emperor and from the provincial governor, and decrees of the League, expounding the honours conferred upon him and his benefactions to his own and other cities. To Rhodiapolis itself he gave temples of Fortune and Nemesis, though these are no longer identifiable. Some 70 yards below to the south is a neat structure of small stones and mortar still 20 feet high, which has recently been illicitly dug;

inside against the back wall is a broad base 5 feet high which carried statues, dedicated by Opramoas, of his father Apollonius and his mother Aristocila.

On the summit of the hill is a building, apparently a tower, some 17 feet square, which until recently stood nearly complete to a height of 15 feet; it has now been largely demolished, and only one wall remains erect. Above the theatre to the west are the ruins of a good-sized church, but only the apse is standing. There is no running water on the site, but many cisterns, some of them very large and of varying shapes, round, rectangular, and sausage-shaped, and some distance to the north-west are some piers of an aqueduct. Close to the tomb of Opramoas are the remains of a stoa, and beyond it another, apparently dedicated by Opramoas himself, but there is not much to be seen.

On the east and west slopes are groups of sarcophagi of Lycian type, and in the rocks around are a number of rock-tombs, some plain, some well built; a few of the latter carry inscriptions, including two in Lycian.

GAGAE

Gagae lies to the south-east of Kumluca a mile or so beyond the village of Yenice, on a hill 600 feet high now separated from the sea-shore by half a mile of flat sandy ground. The city is in three parts, an upper and a lower acropolis and the inhabited city on the plain. The road from Kumluca to Antalya passes comparatively close; at a point 10 miles from Kumluca a forestry road branches from it to the right and leads to within a short climb of the summit.

For the antiquity of Gagae we have the circumstance mentioned above that the title 'Lycian' appears on its federal coins; its earliest appearance in literature is a mention by the pseudo-Scylax in the fourth century B.C. For what it is worth, the city is also said to have been called Palaion Teichos, or Old Castle. Of its foundation two stories are told, more picturesque than convincing. The first relates that certain Rhodians, desiring land in Lycia on which to settle, expressed their wishes to the natives by shouting 'ga, ga', that is 'land, land', *ga* being the Doric form, used at Rhodes, of *ge*; when their wish was granted, they named the new city accordingly. The second, more circumstantial, account says that a Rhodian commander Nemius, after winning a sea-battle over the pirates of Lycia and Cilicia, ran into a storm and his ship was in danger; when the crew sighted land, they cried out 'ga, ga', put into shore, and were saved. Next day he founded a city and called it Gaga. The only value that these tales may be thought to have is that they agree in attributing the foundation to Rhodians.

Although Gagae is called by Eusebius 'a not undistinguished city of Lycia', it is in fact chiefly noted for a mineral said to be found in its neighbourhood and called *gagates*; this is the origin of the word 'jet', though in the ancient authors who speak of it, it is more often a combustible substance resembling lignite. Oddly, these authors speak of a river Gages in addition to the city, though in fact there is no river nearer to Gagae than the Alâkır; Galen writes with more authority, 'As for myself I have not seen this river, though I have coasted along the whole of Lycia in a small boat to acquire knowledge of the country'. As regards the nature of the *lapis gagates* it is at least agreed to have been black, but it is not to be found on the spot today; Spratt observes that 'there is no peculiarity in the mineral character of the surrounding country, which is composed of serpentine, porphyritic traps, and nummulite limestone'. The site is indeed known as 'White Stone', Aktaş, from a white rock 30 feet high between the city and the sea.

The upper part of the hill is enclosed by a ring-wall of small stones fitted with mortar. It has a gate 5 feet wide on the west side near the north end, which has at some time been repaired; there is a deep hole in the upright to receive the bar by which the gate was closed. It is approached only by a steep and narrow path. On the summit is a tower some 50 feet long by 25 feet wide; its wall is of rather irregular bossed ashlar (Pl. 88), with a short polygonal stretch at one corner. Some half-dozen courses are standing to a height of about 10 feet. There is a dividing wall across the middle. Running north-east from this tower is a wall of similar masonry some 30 yards long, leading to a semicircular structure with three or four rows of seats, rather like the synthronon of a church. The nature of this building is not clear.

L

About half-way down the hill on the side towards the sea, visible from the summit, is the lower acropolis. It has a precipice on one side, and the others are defended by the natural rock supplemented where necessary by a solid wall. There is nothing of interest in the interior.

On the plain Spratt saw 'considerable' ruins of Roman and medieval date: several substantial buildings, some Christian churches, and even 'the walls of the town', as well as detached portions of an aqueduct of brick and small stones extending towards Yenice. Of all this hardly anything remains to be seen today; but in 1960 the present writer was surprised to find the emplacement of a small theatre at the north-west foot of the hill. The building has now gone, apart from the hollow in the hillside and some carved blocks, one or two still in position; but the guide who pointed it out, and claimed to have dug it himself, spoke of rows of seats, and in 1972 another villager, born and bred in the neighbourhood, said that thirty years ago the theatre was 'complete'. Like Corydalla, Gagae has been carried off stone by stone to serve the needs of the local inhabitants.

PHASELIS

The east-coast cities of Olympus and Phaselis were described in *Turkey's Southern Shore*. Since that book appeared, however, German scholars have conducted investigations at Phaselis which, even without excavation, have yielded new discoveries and better understanding of the ruins as a whole, also a much more accurate plan of the site, from which Fig. 17 is, with their kind permission, adapted. The chief amendments needed to my earlier account may be briefly stated.

The main street of the city, the paved avenue, is not continuous but falls into two parts set at an oblique angle; the gap between them was perhaps filled by a small square. The northern part is flanked on the west by a row of small rooms, shops, or places of business; there are some indications of a similar row on the east side. To the west of the southern part are three buildings, all of which appear to be agorae. The northernmost (G) is identified by an inscription as the Rectangular Agora, of Hadrianic date; adjoining it on the west

A. North Harbour
B. Central Harbour
C. South Harbour
D. Main Avenue
E. Gate of Hadrian
F. Theatre
G. Rectangular Agora
H. Agora of Domitian
J. Agora
K. Baths(?)
L. Aqueduct
M. City Wall
N Outer Fortification
P. Gate
Q. Temple
R. Cistern

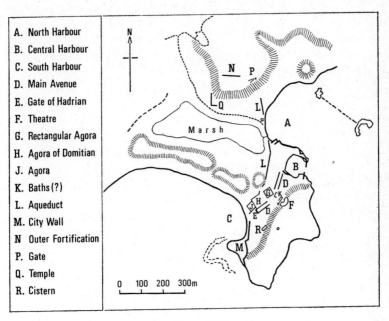

FIG. 17 Plan of Phaselis

is a small church of basilica-type added much later. The middle building (H) is a large open space bordered by chambers on east and south. On the east side, bordering the street, the space between the first two chambers from the north is spanned by an arch still standing complete, and over the door of the third chamber is an inscription with the name of the emperor Domitian (A.D. 81–96). The southernmost of the three agorae (J) is not earlier than Byzantine. At the south end of the northern avenue is a building (K) comprising a number of rooms which may be a small baths. Another bathhouse, of later date, is included in the complex of buildings behind and partly overlying the row of chambers lining the northern avenue. The theatre proves on closer examination among the forest in which it is buried to have the normal five doors at stage-level, and a row of six small doors at orchestra-level. Further down the hillside on the south-west are remains of an angled stairway by which the theatre was approached from the avenue. The

theatre itself was in existence certainly by the second century
A.D.; whether it replaced an earlier Hellenistic building is
uncertain.

But the most interesting discovery made by the German
investigators is that of a fortified settlement on the hill
immediately to the north. It occupied the slope above the marsh
and the level ground higher up, and was enclosed by a wall of
Hellenistic masonry which is best preserved at the points
marked (M) and (N) on the plan; a tower and three archery-slits
in the wall confirm its military nature. At (P) is the entrance to
the enclosure by way of a road cut in the rock, and to the east
of this are the half-buried remains of a rock-sanctuary. Other
walls, now barely traceable and not shown on the plan, run to
the north. Inside the south-west angle of the enclosure (Q) is a
foundation over 60 feet long which is likely to be that of a
temple, but without excavation nothing more can be said of it.
In the north-east part of the enclosure is the spring which fed
the aqueduct. The purpose of this northern fortification, and in
particular of its extension down to the edge of the marsh, is not
altogether clear; most likely it was intended to prevent the
approach of an enemy between the marsh and the sea.

Other points of interest are the quay wall in the small central
harbour, with projecting bollards at intervals, and traces of an
ancient road to the west of the city (west of marsh on the plan).
Except for the walls of the northern settlement everything on
the site is of Roman or Byzantine date.

CHAPTER SIXTEEN

Northern Lycia

THE NORTHERN PART OF LYCIA, of which Elmalı is the modern centre, is of very different character from the rest. Here is by far the largest extent of arable land in the country. The plain of Elmalı falls into two parts, a north-eastern and a south-western; the former is some 12 miles long and 2 to 3 miles wide, the latter rather less extensive owing to the lake which, until it was drained in 1953, occupied much of its area. Despite its obvious advantages for agriculture this region seems to have had little attraction for the Lycians in early times; it contains two cities, Podalia and Choma, both of which were apparently included in the Lycian League under the Empire, but nothing is heard of them before the late Hellenistic age. A handful of rock-tombs just beyond the limits of the plain on the west and south-west, and a large hoard of Lycian staters found between the Avlan Gölü and the modern highroad, are the only clear evidence of early Lycian interest in these parts, except for two fine painted tombs recently discovered near Elmalı, one at Kızılbel, the other at Karaburun, dated by their American excavator to the late sixth and early fifth centuries respectively.

PODALIA

Whereas the site of Choma has recently been determined with complete certainty by inscriptions found on the spot, for Podalia the same evidence is not available. Consequently a variety of suggestions has been made, of which the one that has hitherto found most favour locates Podalia at an ancient site on the north shore of the Avlan Gölü.[1] Here is a rocky scrub-

---

[1] Hence the hoard of coins mentioned above is generally called the 'Podalia hoard'.

covered hill of moderate height, in two parts joined by a saddle; on the northern part are the remains of a ring-wall standing up to 10 feet high in fairly regular ashlar masonry, and on the summit a collapsed building of small stones, a tower or small citadel. Rather less than half-way up the north-east slope are two small rock-tombs, but they are not of Lycian type. In the interior are considerable quantities of uncut building-stones, but no squared blocks nor any marble; here and there traces of slender walls are visible. The pottery is of Hellenistic and later date. On the flat ground at the foot of the hill are some indications of ancient occupation, though nothing above ground-level; here a few sherds of Early Bronze Age date have been picked up.

The identification of this site with Podalia was made by Eugen Petersen in 1882. He was greatly strengthened in his belief by finding that the Turks in Elmalı knew it as Podalia, or occasionally Podamia. Since no one had previously identified it with the ancient Podalia, Petersen rightly observed that the locals could not have learned the name from modern scholars visiting the region, so that it must be a genuine survival.

Despite this evidence the present writer has never felt altogether satisfied with this identification. The site at Avlan Gölü does not appear to have the characteristics of a city-site, but rather of a military fortification. In particular, the total absence of any carved stones or inscriptions is noticeable—the latter especially so, since inscriptions are normally abundant on Lycian city-sites.[2] It may also be remarked that Avlan Gölü is only 6 miles from Choma, so that we should have the two cities of the region standing close together at its southern end, leaving the northern part of the plain of Elmalı blank. It seemed that if a suitable site could be found in this northern part, we should have a more satisfactory state of affairs.

Such a site does in fact exist, at the village of Söğle about 8 miles south-east of Elmalı. On the occasion of a visit in 1965 the writer found there all the signs of civilization and urban life which are so conspicuously lacking on the Avlan Gölü site. Just above the village is a rounded hill, low on the north side

[2] The chief exception is Gagae, where only a single inscription has been found, though happily it names the city.

but falling away on the east and south, thickly strewn with sherds ranging in date from the Early Bronze Age through the Iron Age to Hellenistic, Roman, and Byzantine. There are no other remnants of antiquity on the hill, but the village is full of ancient stones. These include altars and other carved blocks, epitaphs, and dedications to gods and emperors; there are also several Byzantine fragments. That this site represents Podalia the writer himself feels no doubt. Here we have a genuine city-site in a satisfactory situation and with a long tradition; the site of Choma being fixed with certainty, what can it be but Podalia? The inscriptions are of Roman date, and the Byzantine fragments prove at least the existence of a church; Podalia was a bishopric in Byzantine times. The lack of a fortification wall such as that at Avlan Gölü is no real obstacle; Choma and even Arycanda are equally undefended.

There remains the difficulty that Petersen in 1882 found the name Podalia actually applied to the ruins at Avlan Gölü. He heard also of an alternative Podamia, and on the Turkish maps a third form appears, Buralye. Now Podamia—that is Potamia, 'river town'—is quite a different matter. It is a very natural name for a place situated just where the Akçay, the only considerable river of the region, enters the lake. In the hope of clearing up the uncertainty the present writer in 1967 made enquiries among the neighbouring villagers, particularly at Karamık, the nearest village to the site. Here, after the usual polite exchange of questions concerning on the one side the village school, the crops, and the quality of the water, and on the other side the visitor's age, salary, and marital status, the conversation proceeded: 'Tell me about the ruins on the hill over there; what name do you give them?' 'Asar' (the stock name for an ancient site). 'On the map here it says Buralye'. 'Ah, no, not Buralye, Budalye'. 'And Budamye?' 'Yes, some people say Budamye, but Budalye is better'. The villagers' preference for Budalye is of course natural at the present time, since the site has been known to scholars as Podalia for ninety years, and they must often have heard the name; yet the alternative Bodamia still persists, and indeed is heard, as the writer was informed, elsewhere in the neighbourhood of Elmalı. It is hard to resist the conclusion that the original name was

Potamia, having no connexion with Podalia at Söğle on the other half of the plain. But the puzzle of the two forms will remain.

CHOMA

Concerning the site of Choma there is no such problem, though it has only recently been determined. In and around the villages of Hacımusalar and Sarılar, some 9 miles south-west of Elmalı, R. M. Harrison in 1963 found a series of inscriptions, half a dozen of which gave the name either whole or in part. One is a decree of the Council and People of Choma, another records the erection of an exedra with statues, others are epitaphs; with one possible exception none is earlier than the Roman Imperial age.

Choma is a Greek name, meaning 'mound', and the reason for its adoption is immediately evident to anyone who visits the place. Rather over a mile south-east of Hacımusalar is a large prehistoric mound of the type known as *hüyük*; though of no great height, it is conspicuous in the dead flat plain which extends for miles around. Standing on the mound and looking westward in a favourable evening light, it is possible to make out the rectangular outlines of the city 'blocks' among the fields. On and around the mound a few sherds of Roman date are scattered. Of the city itself nothing whatever remains. The river Akçay passes the site a short distance to the south; according to Pliny its ancient name was the Aedesa.

Less than 3 miles to the north-west of Choma, in the hills some forty minutes' walk above the village of Kızılca, is a pair of Lycian tombs cut in a rock-face; it is unlikely that they belong in any way to the city of Choma, which may well not have existed when they were cut. One is uninscribed, the other has a Lycian inscription in two parts. This is by far the most northerly inscription in the Lycian language yet discovered, and is one of the very few indications of early Lycian concern with this country. Its other point of interest is that it ends with the words *kñtawata* [*p*]*ericlehe*, of which mention was made above in connexion with Limyra, capital of the dynast Pericles in the fourth century. Curiously, Stephanus of Byzantium describes Podalia as 'near Limyra', which on any showing it is not. What

86 Rhodiapolis. Characteristic style of masonry.

89 Nisa. Sarcophagus.

87 [*opposite*] Rhodiapolis. Theatre.

88 [*opposite*] Gagae. Early wall on summit.

90 Northern Lycia. Lion Tomb.

91 Balbura. Supporting wall of Theatre.

93 Kozağacı. Relief on hillside.

92 Kozağacı. Reliefs on hillside.

95 Oenoanda. City-wall.

94 Kozagacı.

96 Oenoanda. Polygonal wall.

led him to make this statement we cannot know, but is it fanciful to see here evidence that Pericles extended his power to this northern country?

Nine miles to the north-west of Elmalı, at the village of Güğü, now officially Yapraklı, is a small ancient village-site. The road from Elmalı is the former highroad to Fethiye; the writer traversed it in a taxi in 1953, but it is now, in spite of repairs, still very rough. The Güğü ascent is indeed barely passable at all. A visit is worthwhile chiefly for a series of rock-cut stelae with reliefs a short climb above the village; the spot is known as Buzağı Kaya from the buffalo represented on one of them. The stelae are dated by their inscriptions to the Hellenistic period. An epitaph of Lycian type on a sarcophagus lid in the village indicates that the place was called in antiquity Orpeëni.

On the north side of Elmalı Dağı, half an hour above the village of Macun, is another small site, only recently discovered and without any specifically Lycian features. It has a tiny acropolis on a hill low on the north but falling away on the south, with a ring-wall of dry rubble with very rough ashlar in places. The other antiquities are sepulchral. Most notable are two sarcophagi with recumbent lions on the lid (Fig. 18), of the type familiar in the Cibyratis but not in Lycia itself. On a mound near the acropolis are the ruins of a built tomb of handsome, well-cut blocks, two bearing a relief of a shield crossed by a scabbard. Lower down to the north is a sarcophagus cut in a large boulder now overthrown, and lower down again to the east are various reliefs cut on the rocks. Nothing has appeared to indicate the name of this site.

South of Choma the Elmalı plain narrows to a broad valley watered by the Akçay. On the east side of this valley, a mile or so south of the village of Armutlu, is a hill some 500 or 600 feet high carrying a fortress of moderate extent with a ring-wall of very loose polygonal masonry, the interstices being filled with small stones; in one part squared blocks also are used. In the interior are great quantities of uncut building-stones and traces of numerous walls. This site has in the past been suggested as

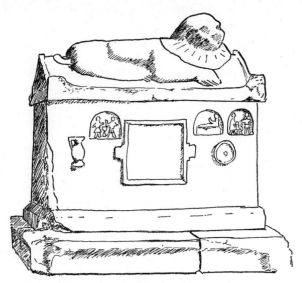

FIG. 18 Tomb with Lion Lid

that of Choma or Podalia, but it seems to be nothing more than a military stronghold.

At the south-west extremity of the same valley is the village of Gömbe, preserving the name of the ancient Comba. Nothing whatever is said of Comba in the ancient literature, apart from the bare mention of its name by the later geographers and in the bishopric lists. It was, however, a genuine city, with a Council and Assembly, though no coinage is known. For whatever reason, Comba was not among the cities that received gifts from Opramoas, whereas Podalia, Choma, and Nisa were.

Comba had, however, one claim to distinction. It was the centre of the cult of the Twelve Gods of Lycia. Over twenty dedications to these deities have been found in various parts of Lycia and elsewhere, eight at least near Comba itself. They consist of a stone slab generally about 3 inches thick and up to 2 feet in length, with a relief of remarkably consistent character. This shows invariably fourteen figures, an upper row containing the Twelve Gods in two groups of six, with a single figure in the middle, and a lower row with a smaller figure between two

groups of animals, apparently dogs. The upper single figure is
usually male, but in two cases female, the figure in the lower row
probably always male. The inscription normally reads: 'to the
Twelve Gods by command', followed by the dedicant's name. In
one case, however (Fig. 19), the dedication is made 'to Artemis,
to the Twelve Gods, and to their father'. An Artemis of Comba
is known from other inscriptions. On this particular stone the
central figure is female, and must surely be Artemis; where it
is male it is presumably the father, and Artemis is not included.
The smaller figure in the lower row is taken in all cases to be
the dedicant. The stone in Fig. 19 has the further peculiarity
that the Twelve Gods carry shields; elsewhere they are dressed
only in tunics. The presence of the dogs indicates that they are
hunting deities. The style of the reliefs is crude and quaint, and
they can hardly date earlier than the third century A.D.

The site of the city is on a high hill above Gömbe on the
south-west, a stiff hour's climb of a thousand feet from the
village. The effort of reaching it is poorly rewarded, as nothing
remains beyond some late walls and a few stones. Some distance
to the east of the hill are the ruins of a church, and in the two
or three houses just below the summit are a number of cut

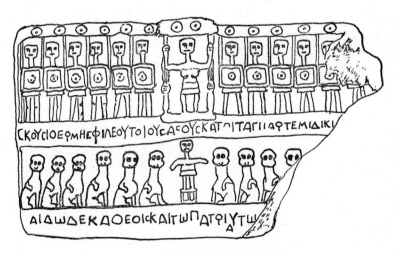

FIG. 19 The Twelve Gods of Lycia

blocks taken from the site. Comba today serves as the *yayla* of
Candyba.

Eight miles to the south of Comba is the city of Nisa, little
known and hardly ever visited. There is a poorish road as far
as Sütleğen, and after that a pleasant walk of something over
an hour. The city is set in the angle formed by the tremendous
gorge of the Akörü Çayı[3] and a smaller stream on the south. The
view is spectacular. As with Comba, all that is said of Nisa in
the ancient writers is a mention by the later geographers,
generally in a corrupted form, and in the bishopric lists. The
site was unknown before 1895; it is proved by inscriptions found
on the spot. No coinage was known until the present writer
obtained in Gömbe a small silver coin of Hellenistic date and
non-federal type inscribed with the name.

The ruins are much overgrown, but a fair amount survives.
The ring-wall, of rough, almost 'Cyclopean' masonry, is best
preserved on the south. On this side also is the theatre, of
medium size, built for the city by two of its citizens not earlier
than the second century A.D. Most of its seats are preserved,
though a good deal disrupted; very little of the stage remains.
Close by on the east is the stadium, with some of its seats in
place; not far away is the statue-base of a local victor in the
games instituted by a distinguished citizen who had attained
the rank of Lyciarch. Just above is a paved terrace which seems
to have been a stoa. Other remains include an arched gateway,
a large building now totally collapsed, and a number of
sarcophagi and built tombs; one (Pl. 89) has two recumbent
figures on the lid.

[3] Often pronounced Ağörü (Ahuri on the old maps).

CHAPTER SEVENTEEN

The Cibyratis

CIBYRA

The city of Cibyra was never at any time a part of Lycia. Its early history is told by Strabo, according to whom the Cibyrates were said to be descendants of Lydians who occupied the region of Cabalis; later the neighbouring Pisidians moved in and transferred the city to a new site, well defended and about a hundred stades in circumference, with a wide territory. Later again the cities of Bubon, Balbura, and Oenoanda joined Cibyra to form a tetrapolis, with Cibyra at its head. The city prospered under a succession of tyrants, and was able to put into the field a force of 30,000 infantry and 2,000 cavalry. We may safely infer a total population well into six figures. By reason of its pre-eminence Cibyra possessed two votes in the assembly of the tetrapolis to one each for the others. Strabo observes further that Cibyra was distinguished for craftsmanship in iron, and that four languages were spoken in the city, Pisidian, Solymian, Greek, and Lydian.

In 189 B.C., following the settlement of Asia Minor after the battle of Magnesia, the Roman consul Manlius Vulso set out with an army for the ostensible purpose of subduing the Galatians who had aided Antiochus; in practice he turned it into a money-raising raid on the cities. At this time Cibyra was under a tyrant by the name of Moagetes, described by the historians as a savage and treacherous man. As Manlius approached, he sent forward a detachment to test the tyrant's reactions. Moagetes declared himself willing to do as the consul wished, and offered a gold crown of the value of fifteen talents, asking him in return to restrain his soldiers from looting the country. On learning the consul's uncompromising response to this optimistic offer, he came next day in person to the Roman camp, humbly dressed and professing great poverty; by stripping himself to the bone he thought he could manage to raise twenty-five talents. Manlius was not impressed: 'Enough of this play-acting; twenty-five talents exhaust your resources? Either you bring five hundred within three days or you may expect your land to be ravaged and your city besieged'. Finally, amid tears and protestations, he agreed to a hundred talents and 10,000 bushels of corn.

By way of illustrating his lack of wealth Moagetes pointed to the poverty of the towns under his control; their names were Syleum and Alimne. Both are utterly obscure, and the names themselves are not free from doubt. It is clear that the tetrapolis was not yet in existence at that time. It was formed at some uncertain date later in the second century and continued to exist until the end of the Mithridatic War about 82 B.C. It was then dissolved by Sulla's lieutenant Murena, who attached Bubon and Balbura to Lycia, leaving Cibyra in the province of Asia. Strabo, who reports this, does not mention Oenoanda, but it too must have gone to Lycia with the others; under the Empire at least it was a full member of the Lycian League.

In the province of Asia, Cibyra was one of the largest *conventus* and a judicial seat of the provincial governor. Destroyed by an earthquake in A.D. 23, it was restored with help from the emperor Tiberius, taking in his honour the name of Caesarea Cibyra, and commencing from A.D. 25 a new dating era.

Cibyra's ruins lie half an hour above the village of Gölhisar (Horzum); a fine street of tombs leads up to the site. The city seems never to have been defended by a wall; perhaps a circumference of a hundred stades, or something like 11 miles, was more than could be managed. It is not in fact clear how the hundred stades were reckoned; the ruins occupy an area barely 1 mile in length and much less in breadth, but even here there is no sign of a ring-wall. The street of tombs leads by a ruined arch to the stadium, which is still in good condition. It is of full size, with a triple entrance arch, now collapsed, at the north end. Some twenty rows of seats are set in the hillside on the

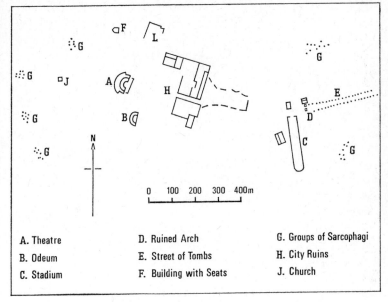

A. Theatre   D. Ruined Arch   G. Groups of Sarcophagi

B. Odeum   E. Street of Tombs   H. City Ruins

C. Stadium   F. Building with Seats   J. Church

Fig. 20 Plan of Cibyra

west; on the opposite side a few rows were built up. The south end is curved in the usual way.

At the other, west, end of the city is the theatre, also in decent preservation. It is of good size, with a single diazoma and between forty and fifty rows of seats, some being buried; of the stage-building two of the doorways are standing complete, also the jambs of another. On the back wall of the diazoma is a series of inscriptions recording honours paid to two brothers, Philagrus and Marsyas, by the five tribes of Cibyra. One of them gives the curious information that the Rhodian drachma was worth at Cibyra only ten asses instead of the usual twelve.

About a hundred yards to the south of the theatre is a smaller theatre or odeum, plain but well preserved. Its front wall contains five arched doors flanked by two rectangular; in the interior a dozen or so rows of seats are visible above ground. Some 200 yards to the north of the theatre is another small building with seats, and many other ruins are scattered over the ground between theatre and stadium, but the site has never been excavated and their identity is not ascertainable. The tombs are mostly sarcophagi, but built tombs are not infrequent.

BUBON

Bubon lies about 15 miles south of Cibyra, some five hours' comfortable walk. The Horzum Çayı needs to be forded, but it is very shallow. The ruins are on a hill called Dikmen Tepe a mile south of the village of Ibecik. Spratt in 1842 found them disappointing; he saw only a walled acropolis, a small theatre of coarse sandstone, and several terraces strewn with the prostrate remains of temples and other buildings. The present writer in 1952 saw much the same, but on a second visit in 1966 found the scene completely changed. The entire slope of the hill had recently been dug from top to bottom by the villagers in search of loot; their pits left hardly a yard of space between them. Of the ruins, such as they were, nothing now remains; but in the course of digging in the theatre a large stone covered with writing was said to have been found. This had become buried again, but a band of villagers was persuaded, for a consideration, to find it and bring it to light. It proved to be well worth the trouble, being a long letter from the emperor Commodus (A.D. 180–192) to the people of Bubon, in which he praises them for their efforts in suppressing the bandits and confirms a decree of the Lycian League raising their status from a two-vote to a three-vote city. The modest city of Bubon is thus, two hundred years after the time of Strabo, set on a par with Xanthus, Patara, and the other first-class members of the League.[1] The prevalence of banditry in the wilder parts of Asia Minor, especially in the late second and early third centuries, is well known; we hear often of police officers, *stationarii*, installed at guard posts by the Roman government to control it, but its suppression was for the most part left to the individual cities, where police, mountain-guards, and keepers of the peace were regularly appointed, with a troop of runners under them. At Bubon, however, there seems on this occasion to have been rather a communal effort by the body of the citizens involving

[1] It appears from the phrasing that three votes was the maximum possible number.

a regular campaign. The stone carrying this inscription appears to be in its original position in the theatre, but it is no doubt buried again by now.

The most interesting thing now to be seen at Bubon is a rock-cut tomb just outside Ibecik on the north, close beside the road. It is very simple, a good deal damaged, and not of specifically Lycian type. It has a porch with two very rough Ionic columns; the door has uprights and pediment in relief, though mostly broken away. Inside is a bench for three corpses; the roof is roughly arched. The tomb has an aspect of great antiquity, which is perhaps misleading. It has no inscription.

Bubon was mentioned above in connexion with Araxa (p. 70). From the inscription there referred to we learn that at some time in the second century B.C. war broke out between Araxa and 'Moagetes and the Bubonians'; the Araxans sent an envoy to Cibyra to denounce the Bubonians and secured a satisfactory settlement. Whether or not the tetrapolis was in existence at the time, it appears that Cibyra had some influence at Bubon. After this, however, Moagetes again sent raiders into Araxan territory and carried off a number of its citizens; this time the Araxans appealed to the League. The same man, Orthagoras, was dispatched as envoy in the name of the League both to Bubon and to Cibyra; although neither of these cities was Lycian, the ambassador was able to fulfil his mission 'in a manner worthy of the city and the Lycian nation'. The actual terms of the settlement are not recorded.

The historian Diodorus writes of a distinguished Bubonian who about 145 B.C. was appointed general and acquired such power that he was able to make himself openly tyrant. After a while his brother, desiring the power for himself, killed him and succeeded to his place. The dead tyrant's children were secretly removed to Termessus, and on coming to manhood revenged their father by slaying the usurper; disdaining the tyranny, they restored democracy to their city. The tyrant's name is given variously in the manuscript as Molkestes, Mokeltes, or Molketes; the conjecture Moagetes has been made and widely accepted, and it has further been suggested (though with less approval) that this may be the same man who features in the

M

Araxan inscription. The question depends largely on the date of the inscription, which is not yet finally agreed.

BALBURA

Balbura lies 12 or 13 miles to the east of Bubon; the road leads by Dirmil. Rather over an hour from Ibecik, at the summit of the pass, are the ruins of an ancient fort above the road on the left. The spot is known as Asar Tepe. Among a confused complex of dry rubble walls is a ruined building of some size close to the road; in this are lying two altars with dedications to Ares. The fort commands the pass, which seems to mark the boundary between Bubon and Balbura.

Dirmil is not an ancient site, though the village is full of carved and inscribed stones; its ancient representative lies a mile or two to the east on the road to Balbura. Here a small hill or knoll carries remains of ancient walling and several lion-tombs of the type mentioned above (p. 157).

From here the road rises gradually to another pass, after which the ruins of Balbura come into sight on the right of the road. The spot is now known by the curious name Çölkayığı, 'ship of the desert', though no one seems to know why; the name Katara, which Spratt heard, is not now used, though Gadıra is the name of a hill with a chrome-mine some half an hour to the east. The site of the city is abundantly proved by inscriptions, but apart from its membership of the tetrapolis it has no history at all. It is the most loftily situated of all the Lycian cities, the acropolis rising to close on 5,000 feet above sea-level. The ruins lie on two hills, one on either side of a stream which forms one of the headwaters of the Xanthus river.

The northern or acropolis hill carries a ring-wall of polygonal masonry about 6 feet thick; it contains some re-used material and cannot be as early as it looks. On the saddle between this and the adjoining hill is a stretch of wall of dry rubble up to 8 feet high. Rather more than half-way up the south slope of the acropolis hill is a small but highly interesting theatre. It is barely a hundred feet in diameter, and has only sixteen rows of seats, encumbered at present by fallen tree-trunks. Most remarkably, the middle of the cavea is occupied by a great

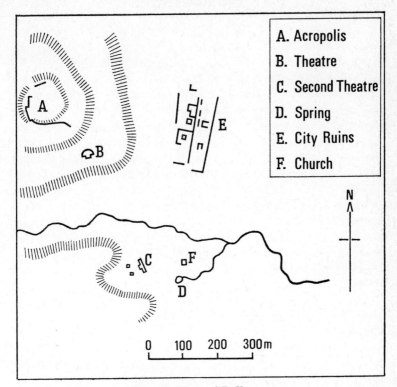

A. Acropolis
B. Theatre
C. Second Theatre
D. Spring
E. City Ruins
F. Church

FIG. 21 Plan of Balbura

projecting mass of rock, left in its natural state and considerably reducing the capacity of the theatre, which in any case is small for the size of the city. Nothing remains of any stage-building apart from a level platform supported on the outside by a wall of most striking appearance (Pl. 91). The masonry is a strongly bossed polygonal of late type, with buttresses of squared blocks, the whole in excellent preservation to its full height. A little way above the theatre are two unusual tombs. In each case a recess of rough outline and about a man's height has been cut in the rock and a sarcophagus sunk in the floor. These tombs are not likely to be of any high antiquity.

At the foot of the southern hill across the stream is a second 'theatre', though it is unlike any other in the writer's experience.

None of the usual features of a theatre are present, only a long solid platform of squared blocks some 50 yards in length, 8 or 9 feet in width and 2 or 3 feet in height, with supporting arches below. In the middle a smaller platform, also raised on an arch, projects towards the hollow in the hillside. The 'cavea' is of the rudest kind; the semicircle of rocks remains for the most part untouched, but here and there a few seats have been cut in them. Less provision for the spectators' comfort could hardly have been made, and it is not likely that the place can have been used for presenting full-length plays; Spratt suggested it may have been 'a place of exhibition for combats of animals'. There is certainly no sign of any stage-building apart from the platform itself, though some wooden structure may of course have been erected on this. The small projecting platform looks like a speaker's rostrum, and it is tempting to imagine that the place was intended for public assemblies or meetings; the theatre, which was commonly used for assemblies in later times, is at Balbura surely too small for the purpose.

The city centre is at the foot of the northern hill. The ruins are abundant, but nothing has remained standing. The main street and the agora, with an arched entrance, are recognizable, and a temple of Nemesis is identified by its dedicatory inscription; it was built 'for his masters'—that is, for the city—by a public slave by the name of Onesimus. Public slaves performed a great variety of more or less menial and routine duties, functioning for example as street-cleaners, town criers, executioners, firemen, and police, but performing also some civil service tasks, accountancy, and other office work. Their remuneration was not generous, though some, like Onesimus, were able to accumulate a reasonable fortune.

Other features on the site include several tombs with lions on the lid, and numerous piles of building-stones on the acropolis hill which were once private houses; an abundant spring on the south side of the stream afforded a perennial source of water, which was supplemented by cisterns on the northern hill.

Balbura had a wide territory, sharing with Oenoanda the plain of Sekiovası and extending on the north-east as far as the lake of Söğüt, the ancient Caralitis. This lake was originally much larger than it is at present; all that now remains of it is a reedy marsh at its west end, where in the season the natives may be seen paddling canoes formed of hollowed tree-trunks and collecting the reeds for fodder. Near what was once the south-east end of the lake but is now a broad plain, at the village of Kozağacı, is one of the most attractive sites in the country. It was only a village, called Toriaeum, and in the second century A.D. stood at the head of a group of five villages termed a *pentacomia*. Inscriptions show that it belonged to Balbura. There are many items of interest in and around the village of Kozağacı, but the feature of the site is the great number of rock-sculptures in the cliffs which rise steeply at the back. Some of these are illustrated on Plates 92–4. They show considerable variety, but are mostly human figures in relief, generally in twos, threes, or larger numbers, carved on the cliffs and on various outcrops of rock. A steep grassy slope leads up obliquely from the village, so that nearly all the monuments are easily accessible. They are of Hellenistic date, and most have an inscription, generally in the form normally used on honorific statue-bases; they are not therefore to be regarded as tomb-stones, but rather as commemorative monuments placed by relatives or friends. Many are in the form of rock-cut stelae, some of which carry only a wreath or rosette, with or without an inscription, others have an inscription only, and a few are quite blank. High up at the top of the slope is a little valley down which a stream flows before falling down the cliff-face in a series of cascades. Here are some pieces of wall, several blocks with lions' paws, and many sherds; and some way up the steep slope on the north side is a little rock-cut sanctuary. Four votive reliefs show an equestrian deity whose horse proceeds in three cases at a gallop, in one case at a walk; the rider carries a club in his right hand raised behind him. A dedication under one of the reliefs shows his name to be Mases, not otherwise known and evidently a local deity; an inscription on a block lying below near the stream records that the sanctuary, or part of it, was constructed by a citizen in the time of Hadrian with contributions from the *pentacomia* and others.

Just outside the village on the north-west is a curiosity which the villagers are always ready, or even anxious, to show to visitors. It is called Hürlektaş, or Echoing Stone, a cleft in the rock which at times emits a loud murmur, presumably depending on the wind; at the time of the writer's visit it was not willing to perform.

OENOANDA

Oenoanda is more easily visited than Bubon or Balbura, as it lies close above the highroad from Korkuteli to Fethiye; the hill is conspicuous from the Sekiovası. The ascent is most conveniently made from the village of İncealiler. Close below the hill and just before crossing the river the main road passes through the site of Termessus Minor, set on two low hills, not more than mounds, one on each side of the road; the spot is called Kemerarası. The site is weak in the extreme, and could never have been founded without the agreement of the Oenoandans. In its inscriptions the city is called Termessus-by-Oenoanda; these, with only one known exception, were set up in Oenoanda itself. The settlement seems to have been made in the third century B.C. as a colony of Termessus Major,[2] but by Roman Imperial times it had in effect been absorbed by Oenoanda. The two mounds are covered with ancient fragments, but no building is either standing or identifiable. A few years ago the first and only inscription was found on the site; it is a long text beginning with a letter from the emperor Hadrian to the People, and refers to the organization of festivals and sacrifices. Despite its domination by Oenoanda, Termessus Minor had its own constitution and magistrates, and struck its own coins under the Empire.

Of Oenoanda nothing is heard before the second century B.C., when it was a member of the tetrapolis headed by Cibyra. What is known of its history was recorded above (p. 162). Surprisingly, only a single coin of Oenoanda has ever come to light, and that dates before the dissolution of the tetrapolis; Imperial coins of the other three members are reasonably common.

The city lies on a high rounded hill steep on all sides but the south. The summit was occupied by a building now in ruins, and a number of cisterns or reservoirs; the public buildings stood on a succession of terraces descending gradually southwards. Northernmost and highest of these is the theatre, a little over

[2] See *Turkey's Southern Shore*, pp. 122–3.

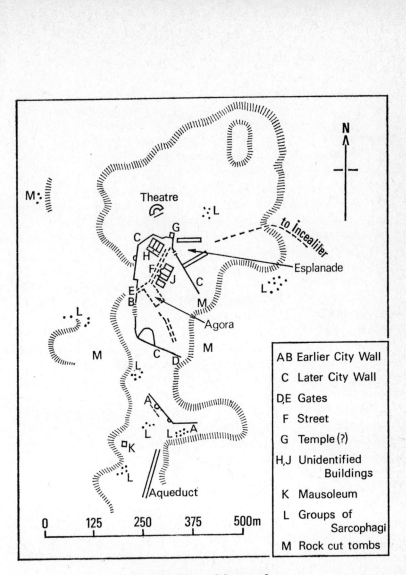

Theatre

to Incealiler

Esplanade

Agora

Aqueduct

A,B	Earlier City Wall
C	Later City Wall
D,E	Gates
F	Street
G	Temple (?)
H,J	Unidentified Buildings
K	Mausoleum
L	Groups of Sarcophagi
M	Rock cut tombs

0   125   250   375   500m

FIG. 22 Plan of Oenoanda

a hundred feet in diameter, with a disproportionately large orchestra; fifteen rows of seats have been counted, with no diazoma. The building is concealed by bushes, and the general state of preservation is not more than fair; Spratt called the proscenium 'very perfect', and in fact several of its small doors are still visible under the collapsed blocks.

The city wall is in two distinct parts. The southern part (A, A on the plan), preserved for a length of 150 yards to a height of 30 feet, is in striking Hellenistic masonry, mainly polygonal and heavily bossed (Pl. 95); it contains two postern gates and two towers, one well preserved, the other ruined. A strongly projecting cornice on the inner face afforded a passage along the wall. Of the continuation of this earlier wall nothing is now to be seen, except perhaps on the west side at the point B, where a short stretch of the later wall appears to be of Hellenistic date. The longer northern part C, C, enclosing the upper portion of the city and standing 10 to 12 feet high in places, is of inferior masonry including a good deal of re-used material; it is of much later date, hardly earlier than the end of the third century. At C a curved inner wall joins the main wall to form an enclosed citadel. Two gates, at D and E, lead in each case to a street.

At the east end of the short north wall, set against its outer face, are the ruins of a small but handsome building G, still 15 feet high, with engaged columns on its north side; a statue and numerous ornamental blocks are lying around. This was evidently a temple, the only one yet identified on the site. At the west end of this wall is a semicircular exedra. Just inside the wall at H is a large building whose purpose is not yet determined; it has an arched façade on its south side. Further to the south is another large structure J comprising three rooms, that in the middle having an apse at one end; the south-west face of this building, in handsome flat-faced polygonal of Roman date, is shown on Plate 96. Immediately adjoining this is a rectangular building in ruined condition, with columns and apparently a water-basin in the middle. To the south again is a level open space which is generally taken to be the agora; the identification is confirmed by the many statue-bases lying in it. The street F, F leading from the gate E crosses the northern

side of the agora and continues to the far side of the city.
Numerous other ruins in this region remain unexplored and
unidentified.

Just outside the existing city wall on the north-east, but
presumably included within the original circuit, is another level
space commonly called the 'Esplanade'. Here also are many
statue-bases. The structures on its north and south sides are
now destroyed, but may have been stoas.

Oenoanda's chief claim to fame lies no doubt in the famous
inscription containing a discourse by the Epicurean philosopher
Diogenes, a native of the city. Very many of the blocks of this
lengthy screed have been found scattered over all parts of the
upper city (Fig. 23), yet it is estimated that only about a third
of the full text has been recovered. If complete it would extend
over a space of 60 yards and would eclipse in length even the
monument of Opramoas at Rhodiapolis. It deals with a great
variety of subjects: the formation of the world, the nature of
images and dreams, the theory of chance, and many others,

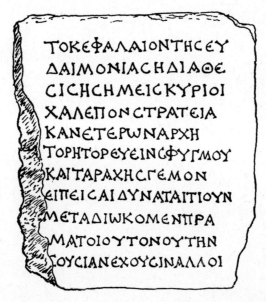

FIG. 23 Oenoanda. A Block of the Diogenes Inscription

from the Epicurean viewpoint, together with a selection of apophthegms, for example:

> The key to happiness is physical condition, a thing in our own control. Military service is hard, even if it gives command of others. Rhetoric, if it can sway opinion, is full of palpitation and confusion. Why then do we pursue a thing whose actuality rests with others?

It is not known with certainty where this egregious inscription was set up, but the latest investigations suggest that it may have stood on a wall on the south side of the 'Esplanade' which crossed the line of the later city wall and was destroyed when that was erected. The blocks of the inscription are most thickly scattered inside and outside the city wall at this point, and some are built into the wall itself.

Tombs at Oenoanda are many and various. Sarcophagi are numerous, some having a recumbent lion on the lid. On the west slope are a few simple rock-tombs and tombs of 'Carian' type, that is a sarcophagus sunk into the rock with a separate lid; in one place, carved on the rock-face, is a human figure in an aedicule and beside it a pair of open hands, the sign of an unnatural or violent death.

But the outstanding tomb on the site is a once handsome mausoleum of marble dating from the second century A.D., now unfortunately in ruin; it lies in a collapsed heap outside the wall on the south-west (к on the plan), not far from the aqueduct. It has a long inscription giving the genealogy of a distinguished Oenoandan family claiming descent from the Spartan Cleander, said to be the founder of Cibyra.[3] The British party at present surveying the site has suggested that this monument might be re-erected from its own blocks, nearly all of which are still on the spot.

An attractive excursion for those with the time to spare is a walk from Oenoanda to the lake of Girdev Gölü, on the high ground to the south-east. The distance is about 12 miles, which in 1952 the writer did on foot with a slow donkey in five hours; a jeep could probably do it quite comfortably. From İncealiler the road, or path, leads to the *yayla* of Ceylan, near which is a

---

[3] This hardly agrees with Strabo's account; see above, p. 161.

curiosity known as Kalkantaş, Shield Stone. This is a circular slab of stone 6 feet in diameter and over a foot thick, set in a socket on top of a pile of rocks, sloping slightly backwards; no one seems to know its age or origin, nor yet its purpose, though it has been used as a rifle target. There are said to have been others in the neighbourhood, but these are now smashed.

From Ceylan begins the ascent, long but gradual and quite easy walking; it reaches over 6,000 feet at its highest point, after which there is a rather steep and stony descent to the lake. This is shallow and formed apparently entirely of melted snow, and is said to dry up in August. It lies in a bowl completely surrounded by hills, and has extensive pastures around it; in summer some two hundred families settle here, drawn from many different villages; the writer's host came from Düver (Tlos) in the Xanthus valley. In the lake is a slightly raised piece of ground which has been enclosed with a wall, with numerous interior walls and foundations of houses. To the north and west of the lake are lying a number of ancient blocks and sarcophagi, some with lion-lids. The antiquities here are not remarkable, but the place itself is very green and pleasant, and the air at this altitude is delightful, though the nights are chilly. Accommodation, in black goats'-hair tents, is primitive in the extreme, but the writer at least was most hospitably entertained.

An inscription on one of the tombs makes the fine for its violation payable to Oenoanda, and the place appears to be a summer village attached to that city. It is perhaps possible to hazard a guess at its ancient name. In the new inscription found at Termessus Minor is a list of villages which are to participate in the sacrifices; one of these is Elbessus, and in the inscription at Güğü mentioned above, a man is said to have come from Elbessus to settle in Orpeëni (see above, p. 157). The mountain just to the north of Girdev Gölü bears the name Elbis Dağı, which must surely be a survival of the ancient name. Elbessus is otherwise quite unknown, as is the name of the site at Girdev Gölü, and it is tempting to bring the two together. But this is admittedly conjectural.

Girdev Gölü may also be reached from Gömbe in about six hours on foot.

★

The Xanthian Stele ('Obelisk')

IN FORM A STRAIGHTFORWARD PILLAR-TOMB, this monument carries on the four sides of the shaft an inscription of over 250 lines which is much more than an epitaph. It is in three parts: (a) a long text in normal Lycian covering the whole of the south and east sides and the upper part of the north; (b) a twelve-line epigram in Greek; (c) a text in the secondary form of Lycian which is almost certainly poetic; this occupies the bottom of the north side and the whole of the west.

The Greek portion is of course immediately intelligible; it records that the 'stele' was dedicated to the Twelve Gods in the agora (where it still stands) in commemoration of war and victories. The owner's name is unfortunately illegible, as it is also in the Lycian; he is son of Harpagus, was a champion wrestler in his youth, sacked many cities with the help of Athena, gave a share of his kingdom to his relatives, slew seven Arcadian hoplites in one day, set up a record number of trophies to Zeus, and by his splendid exploits adorned the family of Karikas.

In the Lycian portions it was observed very quickly after the text was first copied by Fellows that there occur a number of names which are known to Greek history: ATÃNA-Athenian, SPPARTAZI-Spartan, CIZZAPRÑNA-Tissaphernes, ÑTARIYEUS-Darius, MILASÃÑTRA-Melesander, HUMRKKA-Amorges, and others. These, especially the last two, at once fixed the approximate date of the inscription to the latter part of the fifth century. Melesander, as we learn from Thucydides, was sent by Athens with six ships in the winter of 430–429 to collect tribute from the Lycians; he landed and moved inland with an army of men from the ships and from the allies, but was defeated in a battle and killed. Amorges was a Persian who had defected from the King and had established himself in Iasus; in 412 the Spartans, on the advice of the Persian satrap Tissaphernes, attacked him there by sea and captured the city.

It was likely therefore that the Xanthian Stele would have much to tell us of the history of the period; but for a long time the language guarded its secrets. It is indeed only in the last forty years or so that, thanks to the work of scholars, notably Dr Friedrich König and Professor Hans Stoltenberg, the text has become reasonably intelligible. It proves to consist of a long series of honours and dedications made by or to the son of Harpagus and members of his family; in some cases the historical occasion is related in some detail. The hero himself is described as brother of Keriga (Karikas in the Greek) and nephew of Cuprlle; a more remote relative is Teththiweibi; all of these are known from the coins as dynasts. There occur also numerous place-names, some readily identifiable from their Greek equivalents, such as Pttara, Trusa; others identifiable but different from the Greek, such as Arñna-Xanthus, Zemtiya-Limyra; others again quite unknown, such as Tuminehi, Zagaba.

The Xanthian version of the Melesander incident contains some surprises. The Lycians, we find, were by no means united at the time; the defeat of Melesander was achieved by the Xanthians under their leader Trbbenimi, also known from the coins, and Melesander was assisted by the Tloans. At the same time Xanthus, aided by Limyra, was at war with Patara, Zagaba, and Tuminehi; these too, it seems, were supporting Melesander.[1] From this difficult situation Xanthus was saved by campaigns conducted under the supreme command of the son of Harpagus. Tlos was punished for her part in the affair by a Xanthian army under Kerẽi, yet another dynast known from the coins.

With regard to the affair of Amorges, the Xanthian text speaks of a victory of Tissaphernes and the Spartans over the Athenians and Amorges at Iasus. In this the Lycians evidently

---

[1] They and the Tloans must also, apparently, be the 'allies' of which Melesander's force was partly composed. Athenian 'allies', in the time of the Confederacy of Delos, means normally the subject cities which were members; but there is nothing in Thucydides to suggest that any of these were present—unless the Lycians themselves are so reckoned.

played a part, for we learn that 'the authorities' entrusted the preparations for the campaign to Tissaphernes, who subsequently erected a monument in Xanthus to the son of Harpagus. All this is quite different from Thucydides' narrative; it appears to refer to a land campaign by the Lycians (and others?) under Tissaphernes, of which Thucydides says nothing. If this was combined with the Spartan attack by sea, his silence is surprising. Alternatively, it may possibly have occurred earlier. In 412 the Spartans, after capturing Iasus, surrendered Amorges to Tissaphernes. This was the occasion, no doubt, on which the son of Harpagus slew seven Arcadians in a day; we know from Thucydides that Amorges' forces consisted largely of Peloponnesian mercenaries.

The victory over Amorges was won with the help of the god Turakssa, whose name in Greek is Apollo Thyrxeus. The Greek epigram, on the other hand, refers to many successes won with the help of Athena; this is at first sight surprising, when Lycians and Athenians were at enmity. The Lycians were never willing members of the Delian Confederacy, and had not been paying their tribute, which Melesander was sent to collect by force; and still in 412 Amorges and Iasus were holding out for Athens. Nevertheless, it is a fact that the coins of the dynasts, including Keriga and Kerẽi, of the latter part of the fifth century regularly bear the head of Athena on the obverse, and some of them even have her owl as well. By the end of the century better relations were established; and indeed, the mention in the first section of the text of the generals of Darius and Artaxerxes, for whom 'Termilic honours' were decreed at Xanthus, seems to show that the obelisk cannot have been set up much before 400; Artaxerxes II reigned from 405 to about 360.

Bibliography

GENERAL

C. Fellows, *Lycia* (London 1840).

T. A. B. Spratt and E. Forbes, *Travels in Lycia* (London 1847).

O. Benndorf and G. Niemann, *Reisen in Lykien und Karien* (Vienna 1884).

E. Petersen and F. von Luschan, *Reisen in Lykien und Kibyratien* (Vienna 1889).

R. Heberdey and E. Kalinka, *Bericht über zwei Reisen in SW Kleinasien* (Vienna 1897).

Freya Stark, *The Lycian Shore* (London 1956).

Freya Stark, *Alexander's Path* (London 1958).

Hachette's World Guides, *Turkey* (Paris 1960).

E. Akurgal, *Ancient Civilizations and Ruins of Turkey* (Istanbul 1973).

SPECIAL

CHAPTER II

PREPIA: A. Maiuri in *Annuario* IV–V, 419ff.; L. Robert, *Études Anatoliennes*, Chapter XXX; P. Roos in *Opuscula Atheniensia* IX, 68–70.

CALYNDA: J. Arkwright in *JHS* XV, 97; G. E. Bean in *JHS* LXXIII, 25–6; Roos, op. cit., 72–4.

DAEDALA: Roos, op. cit., 91–2.

CRYA: P. M. Fraser and G. E. Bean, *The Rhodian Peraea* (Oxford 1954), 55–6.

CHAPTER IV

LYDAE: J. Bent in *JHS* IX, 83ff.; Roos, op. cit., 75–82.

LISSA: J. Bent in *JHS* X, 50ff.; Heberdey and Kalinka, op. cit., 19; Roos, op. cit., 74.

CHAPTER V

XANTHUS: *Fouilles de Xanthos* (in course of publication);

N

H. Metzger, *Guide de Xanthos* (Ankara 1966), in French and Turkish.

LETOUM: Benndorf and Niemann, op. cit., I, 118f.; H. Metzger in *Revue Archéologique* (1966/i), 101ff.; short excavation reports in *Anatolian Studies* and *American Journal of Archaeology* from 1963.

CHAPTER VI

ARSADA: G. E. Bean in *JHS* LXVIII, 40–6.

ARAXA: Bean, ibid., 46–56.

CHAPTER VIII

PATARA: G. E. Bean, *JHS* LXVIII, 57–8.

CHAPTER IX

PHELLUS: O. Benndorf in *Anzeiger Akad.Wien* (1892), 65; G. E. Bean in *Anzeiger Akad.Wien* (1958), 49–58.

CHAPTER XI

TRYSA: O. Benndorf and G. Niemann, *Das Heroon von Gjölbaschi-Trysa* (1888).

CHAPTER XIII

MYRA: G. E. Bean in *Anzeiger Akad.Wien* (1962), 4–6; *Myra, eine Lykische Metropole*, ed. J. Borchhardt (Berlin 1974).

SURA: G. E. Bean in *Anzeiger Akad.Wien* (1962), 6–8.

CHAPTER XIV

ÇAĞMAN: G. E. Bean in *Anzeiger Akad.Wien* (1962), 8–9. Christian remains: R. M. Harrison in *Anatolian Studies* XIII, 117–51.

CHAPTER XV

LIMYRA: J. Borchhardt in *Archäologischer Anzeiger* (1970), 353–90.

PHASELIS: H. Schläger and J. Schäfer in *Archäologischer Anzeiger* 4 (1971), 542–61.

CHAPTER XVI

PODALIA: E. Petersen, *Reisen in Lykien* II, 161; G. E. Bean in *Anzeiger Akad.Wien* (1968), 157–63, and *Journeys in Northern Lycia* (*Denkschr.Österr.Akad.* 104, 1971), 28–32.

CHOMA: G. E. Bean and R. M. Harrison in *JRS* (1967), 40–4.

NISA, COMBA: R. Heberdey in *Festschrift für H.Kiepert* (1898), 153–8.

CHAPTER XVII

CIBYRATIS: G. E. Bean, *Journeys in Northern Lycia* (1971).

TORIAEUM: Bean, ibid., 18, and *BSA* 51, 152–6.

OENOANDA: A. S. Hall, *Anatolian Studies* XXVI, 191–7.

References

CHAPTER I

P. 20: Hdt. I, 173, cf. Strabo 634, 667. P. 21: Ephorus ap. Strabo 634. P. 21: Apollonius ap. Steph. Byz. s.v. Chrysaoris. P. 22: e.g., Steph. Byz. s.v. Tremile, Strabo 573, 667, 678. P. 23: Etruscans, Hdt. I, 94. P. 23–4: Lycian customs, Hdt. I, 173. P. 24: Lydians, Hdt. I, 28; Harpagus, Hdt. I, 176. P. 24–5: Lycian armour, Hdt. VII, 92. P. 25: Phaselis, Polyaen. 5, 42. P. 26: Antiochus in Lycia, Hieronymus *Comm. in Daniel* XI, 15. P. 26: war with Rhodes, Polyb. XXII, 4, 5, 8, XXIV, 15, XXV, 4, 5, XXX, 5, 31. P. 27: Lycian League, Strabo 664–5. P. 28: Pliny *NH* 5, 97.

CHAPTER II

P. 32: Pliny *NH* 5, 103. P. 33: Pisilis, Strabo 651; Artemisia, Hdt. VIII, 87. P. 34: revolt from Caunus, Polyb. XXXI, 5. P. 35: Daedala, Strabo 651, Livy 37, 22.

CHAPTER III

P. 38: Pericles, Theopompus fr. 111 Muller. P. 38: Alexander, Arrian I, 24. P. 38–9: Nearchus, Polyaen. 5, 35. P. 39: Ptolemy, Livy 37, 56. P. 39: Rhodians, Appian Mithr. 24; Strabo 665, on the other hand, says that when the Pergamene kingdom ended, the Lycians got Telmessus *back*. P. 39: swallow portent, Arrian I, 25.

CHAPTER IV

P. 42: Pliny *NH* 5, 101. P. 42: Cadyanda and Caunus, *TAM* I, 45.

CHAPTER V

P. 49: Strabo 666; Hdt. I, 176. P. 49: Arñña and Xanthus, Steph. Byz. s.v. Xanthos and Arna; Eustathius ad Dionys. Perieget. 5, 129. P. 50: Harpagus, Hdt. I, 176. P. 50: Alexander, Appian *BC* 4, 80; Arrian I, 24; Plut. *Alex.* 17. P. 51: Ptolemy I,

Diod. Sic. 20, 27. P. 51: Antiochus III, *TAM* II, 1, 266.
P. 51–2: Brutus, Appian *BC* 4, 76; Plut. *Brutus* 30–1. P. 56:
Harpies, Homer, *Od.* 20, 66ff. P. 61: Leto in Lycia, Servius ad
Virg. Georg. I, 378; Antoninus Liberalis 35; Ovid *Metam.* 6,
317–81. Syessa, Steph. Byz. s.v. P. 63: Strabo 665.

CHAPTER VI

P. 71: Leto, Quint. Smyrn. 11, 21ff; inscription, *TAM* II, 1,
174.

CHAPTER VII

P. 73: Panyasis 18 ed. Kinkel. P. 73: Pinara—'round', Steph.
Byz. s.v. Artymnesos. P. 73: Pandarus, Strabo 665. P. 73:
Alexander, Arrian I, 24. P. 78–9: Marcian, Cedrenus, *Comp.
Hist.* I, 603, 11ff.

CHAPTER VIII

P. 82: *patara*, Patarus, Steph. Byz. s.v. Patara; Eustathius
ad Dionys. Perieget. 5, 129; Servius ad Virg. *Aen.* III, 332;
Strabo 666. P. 82: Telephus, *Lindische Tempelchronik* B 48;
Menaechmus ap. Steph. Byz. s.v. Telephios. P. 83: oracle, Hdt.
I, 182, Mela I, 82. P. 83: Apollo on Delos, Servius ad Virg. *Aen.*
IV, 143. P. 83: Danaus, Servius ad Virg. *Aen.* IV, 377. P. 84:
Opramoas, *TAM* II. 905, XIII C, XIV E, XVII E. P. 84:
Phocion, Aelian *VH* I, 25. P. 84: Antigonus and Demetrius,
Diod. Sic. 19, 64 and 20, 93. P. 84: Mithridates, Appian *Mithr.*
27. P. 84–5: Brutus, Appian *BC* 4, 52; Plut. *Brutus* 32; Dio
Cassius 47, 34. P. 85: harbour, Appian *BC* 4, 81.

CHAPTER IX

P. 92: bilingual, *TAM* I, 56; Habesos, Pliny *NH* 5, 100.
P. 94: sponges, Pliny *NH* 31, 131. P. 96: Hecataeus ap. Steph.
Byz. s.v. Phellos. P. 97: Phellus inland, Strabo 666, Ptolemy V,
3, 3. P. 99: Sebeda, Alex. Polyh. ap. Steph. Byz. s.v.

CHAPTER XI

P. 107: Candyba, Pliny *NH* 5, 101; Candybus, Steph. Byz.
s.v. P. 109: Jason, *IGR* III, 704.

CHAPTER XII

P. 119: xomendys, *Reisen* II, 47, no. 85, cf. Bean–Mitford, *Journeys in Rough Cilicia 1964–1968* (*Denkschrift Akad. Wien*, 102 (1970)), 175, no. 41.

CHAPTER XIII

P. 120: Const. Porph. *de them.* 14, 37. P. 120: rue, Athen. 2, 59. P. 120: Spinther, Appian *BC* 4, 82. P. 121: ferry service, *OGI* 572. P. 131: fish oracle, Pliny *NH* 32, 17; Plut. *de Soll. Anim.* 23; Athen. 8, 333–4; Steph. Byz. s.v. Sura.

CHAPTER XIV

P. 136: Antiochus III, Athen. 22, 527 F. 'Prow', Sch. ad Pind. *Ol.* 7, 35. P. 136: petition to Maximinus, *TAM* II, 3, 785.

CHAPTER XV

P. 142: Strabo 666, Pliny *NH* 5, 100. P. 143: oracle, Pliny *NH* 31, 22. P. 145: Argive treaty with Xerxes, Hdt. VII, 150–1. P. 148: Palaion Teichos, Alex. Polyh. ap. Steph. Byz. s.v. Gagai. P. 148: legends, Etym. Magn. p. 219; Eusebius *de Mart. Palaest.* 4. P. 149: lapis gagates, Pliny *NH* 36, 141; Galen XIII, 257.

CHAPTER XVII

P. 161: Strabo 631. Moagetes, Livy 38, 14. P. 162: earthquake, Tac. *Ann.* 4, 13, 1.

APPENDIX

P. 177: Thuc. II, 69 and VIII, 28.

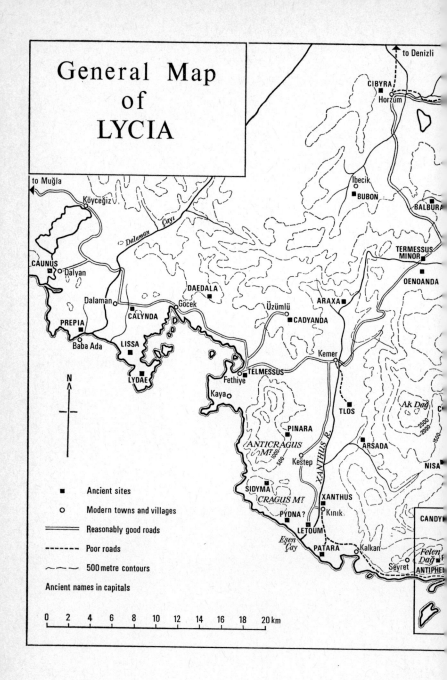

General Map of LYCIA

to Denizli

CIBYRA
Horzum

to Muğla

Köyceğiz

Çayı

Dalaman

Ibecik
BUBON

BALBURA

CAUNUS
Dalyan

DAEDALA

TERMESSUS
MINOR

OENOANDA

Dalaman

CALYNDA

Göcek

Üzümlü
CADYANDA

ARAXA

PREPIA

Baba Ada

LISSA

Kemer

LYDAE

TELMESSUS
Fethiye

Kaya

Ak Dağ

2500
2000
1500

TLOS

PINARA

ANTICRAGUS
Mt.
1000

500

Kestep

ARSADA

NISA

SIDYMA

CRAGUS Mt.

PYDNA?

XANTHUS

Kınık

CANDY

XANTHUS R.

LETOUM

Eşen
Çay

PATARA

Kalkan

Seyret

Felen
Dağ

ANTIPHE

N

■ Ancient sites

○ Modern towns and villages

── Reasonably good roads

---- Poor roads

⌒⌒⌒ 500 metre contours

Ancient names in capitals

0   2   4   6   8   10   12   14   16   18   20 km

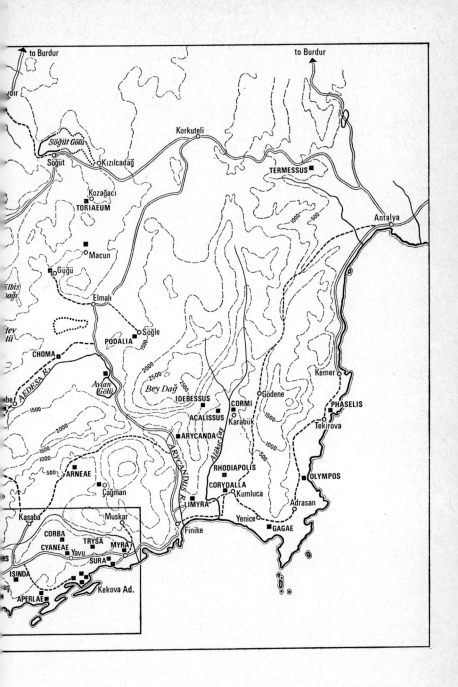

Index

Ernes 134, 135
Etruscan 23
Eudemus 27, 65
Eusebius 149

Faustina the elder 130
Felendağı 96, 97, 98
Felen-Demre river 99, 105
Fellows, Sir Charles 5, 49, 64,
    65, 77, 96, 124, 125, 136,
    177
Fethiye 5, 32, 42
Finike 5, 142
Fortune 147

Gadıra 166
Gagae 143, 146, 148, 150
Gages 149
Gaius Caesar 143, 145
Galen 149
Gâvur Ağlı 63
Gâvuristan 106
Gâvuristanlık 140
Gelemen 106
Gendeve 107, 108
Germanicus 120
Girdev Gölü 174, 175
Glaucus 24
Göcek 32
Gödeme 134
Göksu 142
Gölbaşi 112
Gölhisar 162
Gömbe (Comba) 158, 159, 160,
    175
Gordian III 94, 96, 102, 108,
    121, 135, 139
Güceymen Tepesi 134
Güğü 157, 175

Habesos 93, 97
Hacımusalar 156

Hacıoğlan 100
Haciveliler 146
Hadrian 130, 169, 170
Halicarnassus 39, 40
Harpagus 55, 177, 178, 179
Harpy Tomb 31, 56
Harrison, R. M. 156
Hattusas 21
Hayıtlı 119
Hecataeus 96, 146
Hecate 81
Hecatomnid dynasty 42
Helios 136
Hera 56, 61
Herodotus 20, 21, 22, 23, 24,
    49, 50, 73, 83, 89
Hierocles 102
Hinduwa 21
Hittites 20–1
Hızırkâhya 146
Homer 24, 49, 56, 73
Horzum 162, 164
Hoyran 118, 119
Hürlektaş (Echoing Stone)
    169–70

Iasus 178, 179
Ibecik 164, 165, 166
Idebessus 139, 140
Idrias 21
Iliad 24, 114
İncealiler 170, 174
Indus 32, 34
Inlice 35
Iobates 65
Isinda 102, 104–6
Istlada 119

Jason 29, 109, 111, 121
Jews 65
Julian 33

Printed in Great Britain by
The Bowering Press Ltd
Plymouth and London